Essential
F-Words
for Teens

THE 117 THINGS YOU NEED TO
KNOW BEFORE GRADUATION

SCOTT GRATES

Essential F-Words for Teens © Copyright Scott Grates

For more information, email tribeofteens@gmail.com

ISBN (paperback): 979-8-88759-389-0

ISBN (ebook): 979-8-88759-387-6

This book was a generous gift from:

If you would like to purchase a bundle of books below wholesale cost to donate to a graduating class at your local school:

Visit www.tribeofteens.com

Dedicated to my son Tyler Grates. You first gave me
the title I'll forever be most proud of, Dad.

Allow the words in this book to help you accomplish things you
may never have tried if it weren't for my encouragement.

You are an amazing young man with unlimited
potential. Believe that, now and forever!

Before you start, skip to the end now! Literally the very last page of this book.

Then, rip it out!

My first gift to you is a Super Fancy Bookmark.

Use this bookmark to remember which page you last read, and then keep the bookmark as a reminder of the nine Essential F-Words for Teens.

Ripping a page out of this book at the beginning will also reinforce the fact that this book belongs to you, so make it your own by doing whatever feels right during any given moment.

If you read something you like. . .
- Underline it
- Highlight it
- Star it
- Put a bracket around it

If something you read gives you a thought. . . write that thought on the page.

If you want to expand on my words. . . write down your additional thoughts.

If you don't want to stop reading but want to remind yourself to do something. . . write that reminder in the margin.

If you think something I wrote is stupid. . .
- Cross it out
- Put an X over it
- Write the words, "That's stupid."
- Just don't tell me; I'm a pretty sensitive dude!

Never trust your memory. The more notes you take and highlights you make, the easier it will be to reference your favorite moments from this experience.

Let's do this!!!

Contents

INTRODUCTION

12 Days After You Were Born

October 31, 2005

On the surface, everything was great. A week and five days prior, Mom and I welcomed you to planet Earth. You were a super official human with a birth certificate, a social security number, and a name to go by.

You had two loving parents, four living grandparents, two great grandparents, aunts, uncles and even a dog—who wasn't quite sure what to make of you just yet. Our house was clean; our bills were paid. We had a few bucks in the bank and a bright future ahead.

However, there was one problem. Your father—me—was living a lie. It wasn't a lie to you; it was a lie to myself. You see, I thought I was following the path to success. The yellow brick road to happily ever after. I followed what I believed to be the blueprint for wealth and prosperity. Go to college, get experience, pay your dues, get a better job, gain more experience, pay additional dues, and keep moving up and up and up. To where? Well, I wasn't sure, but I was confident I'd know once I arrived at the place I was meant to be.

However, I was wrong. I was living a lie. Not by design but by default. It was ingrained in me that if I followed this path, I'd have a fancy business card, sit in an expensive office, wear designer clothes, drive a luxury automobile, live in a home with twice as many bedrooms as residents and travel the world only to return to work the following week to keep living the lie I thought would bring me joy.

It was 5:00 in the evening on October 31st, Halloween—your twelfth day on Earth. I was working as a straight commissioned sales representative for a home builder in Northern Virginia, and I was always a "No Plan B" bet on myself kind of guy. I'd either succeed or fail on my own. All in, nothing to lose and everything to prove. At this particular job, the commissions were paid once a month, and commissions were all you received. I worked hard, performed well, consistently met quotas, earned high commissions, and was awarded company trips. My managers earned their commissions and bonuses based on my sales performance. Simply put, the more I earned, the more money my manager made.

Each month I was assigned a goal for the number of homes to sell. If I sold that many homes by the time the clock struck midnight on the final day of the month, everyone would get paid. If not, there would be questions to answer with upper management in the morning.

You were twelve days old. Your mother was amazing, but she was also raising you all alone. I was working long hours with no days off. On October 31st, I was one new home sale away from hitting my goal. It was Halloween, and mom was home alone for the twelfth consecutive night. Trick-or-treaters were ringing the doorbell, the dog was barking, you were crying, your mother was angry, you were hungry, your mother was hungry, the dog was barking, your mother was tired, you were tired, the doorbell was ringing, the dog was barking, and I was at work taking calls from your mother asking when I'd be home.

Your dad needed one more sale at 5:00.

Nothing.

Your dad needed one more sale at 6:00.

Nothing.

Your mom was calling asking when I'd be home. The doorbell was ringing. The dog was barking. You were crying.

Your dad needed one more sale at 7:00.

Nothing.

And that's when my manager called.

Chaos, stress, pressure, expectations, a struggling wife, and a twelve-day-old baby I hadn't met yet. *One* sale away from a *big* bonus.

I answered the phone and was immediately asked the question, "Are you going to make that last sale tonight?"

I answered, "I don't think so."

My manager replied with very few but very direct words that would change the course of our family's history forever, "I don't give a sh*t if you have to sleep in that model home tonight and sell a house to a trick-or-treater. . . *you get it done or else!*"

Silence. . . anxiety. . . hands shaking. . . with shortness of breath, I hung up the phone and knew I was at a crossroads.

Was there any amount of money in the world worth sacrificing everything truly important to me?

At that moment, I realized that after ten years of pursuing money and following the perceived blueprint for success, I had been living a lie.

The next morning, I decided not to explain why I hadn't chosen work goals over family commitments. Instead, I decided to quit my job, reprioritize my life, keep family first and jump into the great unknown against the advice of the masses.

Soon after your birth, your mother and I packed you, the dog, and a few suitcases in the car. We placed a for sale sign in the front yard of our Virginia home and began the drive back to our hometown in New York. We had no place to live and no jobs to work once we arrived.

You were sleeping, and your mother was crying as she asked me, "Are we doing the right thing?"

I answered her honestly, "I don't know."

Crossroad:

You will arrive at points and places in your life that you never expected to be. At times, this will disappoint you. You'll be frustrated and sometimes angry, but you'll have to decide which direction you want to head. The choices you make at specific crossroads will determine the type of life you ultimately live.

At the end of each chapter, I will challenge you to recognize a crossroad. This way, when you arrive at each during your own journey, you'll be aware and prepared to make the best decision in advance.

The story I just shared landed me at a major crossroad. It forced me to understand that all decisions come with a certain level of pain. You'll have to choose to take the short-term pain now or live with a certain level of pain long-term. My advice to you is to take the short-term pain now. Do what's difficult but necessary today so you can move forward in a positive direction tomorrow.

3 Things You Need to Know Before Graduation:

- There is no guaranteed roadmap or blueprint to follow toward success. Everyone's journey is different, as is everyone's definition of success.
- Money is only worth having if you earn it by doing something you enjoy. Don't do something you hate, and sacrifice time with the people you love solely to make more money. If your

goal is to spend more time with the people you love, more money won't help that.

- *Just jump.* . . and then figure the rest out on the way down. You will never be 100 percent ready to do anything. If you are 70 percent certain a change needs to occur in order to move you closer to where you want to be, you're ready to make that change. People's inability and unwillingness to make changes in their lives keep them stuck in places they would rather not be for longer than they should be there.

At the end of each chapter, I will leave you with three things you need to know before graduation. Once you complete this book, you will have consumed all 117 tidbits of knowledge to help better prepare you for your own personal journey.

For the past three decades, I have made countless mistakes, suffered crushing defeats, and failed too many times to mention. This may have you wondering, "Why in the world would I take advice from this dude, then?" Because I have learned from all of it, embraced the concept of *failing forward* and worked like crazy to improve myself continuously.

Through my professional career in the corporate world and extensive efforts coaching my peers, I've learned that the answers we seek today as adults could have been taught to us earlier in our lives. At their core, adults are nothing more than deteriorated teens. We say things like, "If I knew then what I know now, my life would be drastically different." It's true. Had we been armed with better knowledge during our teen years, our lives would be less stressful, more meaningful, and exactly what we envisioned.

So, I write this book for my son Tyler, you the reader, and all teens to create awareness of situations and circumstances when they happen. Sure, you'll make plenty of your own mistakes—and that's a good thing. However, it's the awareness of specific moments, opportunities, thoughts, and feelings that I aim to bring to your attention in the pages ahead.

Please take your time with each short chapter, reflect on your current situation, prepare for the future, and create meaningful conversations with friends, family, coaches, or mentors that are in your life now. Plenty within these pages won't make sense to you at this stage of your life, so I encourage you to revisit those chapters periodically down the road. And finally, don't stop planning, preparing, reflecting, and thinking after you've read the final page.

I'll pause here to acknowledge the fact that at this stage in your life, reading a book may not be your jam—I get it, I truly do. With that in mind, take a quick break and jump online to: www.tribeofteens.com and enter your e-mail on the home page. Each week we will take one small excerpt of this book and do a deeper diver into it via our electronic newsletter. This way you are able to digest the most crucial elements of the book in small, bite-sized pieces each week. We'll also notify you of recently released podcasts featuring your peers as well as ultra-successful adults who will share what they wish they knew when they were your age. Parents, make sure you enter your e-mail to join our tribe as well!

I am outrageously proud of you for taking the time to work through this book. Often, to live the life you want, you must be willing to do the things you don't want to do. The fact that you are taking the time to read this book—right now, in your teens—proves to me you aren't like everyone else. You are truly amazing. Enjoy learning about the nine *Essential F-Words for Teens*, becoming aware of thirty-seven different crossroads in your future, and *The 117 Things You Need to Know Before Graduation*.

SECTION 1
FAILURE

Chapter 1
Why Exams Have Failed You

"The difference between good students and bad students is the good students forget everything five minutes after the test, while the bad students forget everything five minutes before."

~Scott Grates senior quote in the Frankfort-Schuyler yearbook 1995

I was a ten-year-old fifth-grade student in Mr. Conners' class. It was mid-June, and we were taking our final math exam of the year. If I got every answer correct, it would complete my perfect run through fifth-grade math. Yup, I was one test away from scoring 100

percent on every single math exam for the entire year. I felt nervous but confident when I turned my paper in. Patiently I sat for the remainder of the day, and I stayed once all of the students were released. This was common for me. You know the term teacher's pet? I proudly fit that role. I always helped Mr. Conners grade the exams, but he graded mine. Fifty questions, worth two points each. As he went through my exam, I pretended not to watch, but I couldn't help but peek. With great anticipation, I waited to see that 100 percent in red pen atop the exam. It seemed like an eternity. Finally, Mr. Conners wrote my grade and, with a big smile, handed it back to me and said, "Great work once again, Scott! You only got one wrong."

My heartbeat sped up. My stomach tied itself in knots, and a lump formed in my throat. One wrong? How was that possible? I quickly found the question I had answered incorrectly and held back tears as I realized the score was accurate and that the incorrect answer was one I should never have missed. I became dizzy, couldn't speak, and my bottom lip quivered as I quickly exited the room without a goodbye. I lived just three blocks from the school, and I sobbed on the walk home that hot June afternoon. I was devastated. I had failed.

I still remember that day vividly. It's funny how life's journey teaches lessons that you often do not decode until years later. Throughout junior high, I continued to put an outrageous amount of stress on myself to perform at a high level academically, and I did. Then, in my freshman year of high school, I broke down. If I'm being honest, I quit. I didn't quit school; I just quit trying. During my first eight years, I was placed on a pedestal, showcased as the gold standard because my exam scores were higher than most. During my last four years, I was called a failure. Threats were made that I wouldn't be allowed to play sports due to my poor grades. Teachers started telling me I was not college material. Guidance counselors stopped helping; instead, they recommended

I pursue a career as a factory worker rather than pursuing college. I was the same person, with the same potential, but now with different exam scores. My school had a hardline definition of *success* and *failure*.

It wasn't until I entered the corporate world and began to study some of the most successful entrepreneurs and business leaders in the world that I realized *failure is a good thing!*

The truth is standardized testing is what's failing our system. In the real world, rarely are answers simply right or wrong. Most schools teach students *what* to think but now *how* to think. Creativity, problem-solving, and innovation come with exploring the alternatives to what society has deemed the right answer. Without failure, growth cannot happen. Think about that for a second, if there was only one way to do everything, and we all just did it that one way, what would ever change? Nothing. There would be no progress, no advances in medicine or technology, no new products, just daily boredom until the day our lives finally ended. Sounds amazing, right?

Everything positive in the world today is the result of people who understood that failure was the key ingredient to success. Failure is only bad when it's immediately followed by quitting. Admittedly, that's what happened to me when I got to high school; I quit trying—please learn from my mistakes. Instead, have the strength to *fail forward*.

The good news is you were born understanding this concept. You can walk today because you refused to quit when you were a baby. You failed and fell countless times in the beginning. Yet, you instinctively knew to get up and try again. And you did, then you fell, got back up and tried again. Look at you now. You're walking all over the place and never give a second thought to how you'll put one foot in front of the other to successfully move forward.

Honestly, life isn't much different from those early years. Sure, tasks and challenges change, but ultimately our true success is determined by how many times we fall, get back up, learn from the mistake, try again, and move forward. What if walking was an exam in school at the age of one? Well, you probably would have received an F as a grade. The teacher would have moved on to the next lesson, and you would have crawled back to your desk and labeled a failure.

Failure is an essential F-word for your success and long-term happiness in life.

Embrace it.

Allow it to be your greatest teacher.

Don't allow it to scare you from trying something new.

Don't let it hold you down after you fall.

Don't let it define you.

Crossroad:

You'll experience certain moments in life where you've poured significant energy into preparing for a specific event. Perhaps it's a job interview, a presentation, a test, or a relationship. You'll feel ready, confident, and give it your all. And you will fail. You'll then have two choices. Put your head down, pout and cry the entire way home—like I did in fifth grade—or you can re-frame the result. Did you fail, or did you gain a better understanding of what you could have done better? Often the best solution is determined by utilizing a process of elimination. This process will show you ways that certain things won't work so you can ultimately decide what will.

Failing doesn't make you a failure; just be sure to choose the proper direction at this crossroad.

3 Things You Need to Know Before Graduation:

- Success and failure cannot be determined at any point during a journey. It's only at the journey's end that determination can be made. Knowing this, if you never quit, you can never fail.

- The only person who can accurately give you a grade is you. It's up to you to decide the continuous effort you put into something—100 percent effort trumps any letter grade assigned to a temporary result.
- Rarely is there just one answer to a question or one path to arrive at a solution. Life celebrates curious minds.

Chapter 2
Burn the Boats!

"The minute you have a back-up plan,
you've admitted you're not going to succeed."
~Elizabeth Holmes

The concept of "burning boats" is often traced back to a story associated with the conquest of the Aztec Empire by Hernán Cortés. In 1519, Cortés led a large expedition to the new world. The goal was to capture a magnificent treasure said to be held there.

Upon arrival, Cortés destroyed his ships by setting them on fire; *he burned his own boats.* This sent a clear message to his army—no turning back. They would either conquer the Aztec Empire or die trying. However, they could not retreat.

Within two years, Cortés and his army, indeed, conquered the Aztec Empire.

Burning the boats forces you into a point of no return. It gives you no Plan B. It creates a 100 percent psychological commitment to success. Now, it is my deepest wish that you never find yourself in a situation where you will either succeed or die! Yet, I desire you to take this all-in mentality with you throughout your life.

Back to modern times. Perhaps the greatest company slogan ever created came from Nike, "Just Do It." Stories of procrastination, excuses and failure are found in the first chapter of every book written about people who could have, would have, should have, but ultimately didn't. Your life will change forever when you stop talking about making things happen and start to **just do it!**

You will never be completely ready to do anything in your life. Sometimes, you have to jump and figure out your plan on the way down. Taking imperfect action is always better than taking no action at all. And once you take that leap, go all in, and don't look back. Burn your boats.

Please always remember that true failure is never trying something that excites you.

Again, the story of Cortés and his army is a harsh tale of life or death. I use it to emphasize the point of going all-in. However, the choices you'll face in life as you confront your fears will have a far inferior worst-case scenario. In fact, my entire career, I've asked myself a set of questions before taking on a new challenge and jumping into something before I feel completely ready; what is the worst-case scenario here? Will this potentially kill me? Can I potentially end up in prison? Will my family still love and respect me if I fail? As long as the answers to those three questions are no, no, yes, yes—and it's important they are in that order, then I do it. I burn my proverbial boats; I go all in and never look back.

Crossroad:

You will know when the big moments occur in your life when you are faced with a major, potentially life-changing decision to either jump all in or retreat. My challenge to you at this crossroad is to start identifying the moments that aren't as easy to see. We retreat on small, *seemingly insignificant* goals all of the time. Perhaps you skip a workout, make poor food choices, pass on making that call to a family member, or even quit reading a book that can change your life forever—like this one. Understand that retreating from these small goals will compound over time and ultimately keep you from accomplishing your life's big goals.

3 Things You Need to Know Before Graduation:

- Complacency is the enemy of progress. In life, you are either growing or dying. You are improving or regressing. There is no middle. To remain comfortable is to avoid growth and improvement.
- Act on ideas before you are ready, don't seek complete confidence. The world is filled with two types of people, those who talk about making things happen and those who actually do it.
- Four words that will always hold you back are, "I already tried that." Those four words create a false illusion that there's only *one way* to do everything. If you tried it and failed, figure out

a better way and try it again. And potentially again. And potentially again. Your goals in life are far too important to quit on. Never stop trying.

Chapter 3
Fear of Rejection

"If you live for people's acceptance, you'll die from their rejection."
~Lecrae

W e all have fear, but why? Where does it come from? I'm convinced it can be traced back to one deep-rooted, anchor fear that is standard operating equipment within all of us upon birth, **rejection**.

You want people to like you.

You get upset when people criticize you.

You crave acceptance from others.

You don't want to be alone, and you aren't a fan of change.

Rejection validates the lies you tell yourself. For instance, if you don't think you are confident or prepared to take on a challenging task but still try it and fail, that rejection serves as a reminder that you are right. You asked the question or tried the activity and were told no. In your mind, you lost.

So how do we overcome this inherent fear? Think of rejection as a muscle you can train to get stronger. An athlete lifts weights to strengthen muscles. In the beginning, he may be able to bench press one hundred pounds five times. However, after months of training, suddenly, he can bench press one hundred pounds twelve times and do it with ease.

You can reduce your fear of rejection by doing the same. The more you train yourself to face it, the stronger you get, and the less fear lives inside you. If you challenge yourself to do just one thing each day that scares you and will likely lead to rejection, it will become less scary. Then, do two each day. Then, do three. Suddenly after a few months, your fear of rejection is nearly gone. Now you have more confidence and are more likely to take on meaningful work. The more you hear the word no, the less it scares you, and suddenly, the fear of rejection loses its control over you.

Ironically, we spend so many of our younger years fearing rejection and being told no, that we often stop pursuing the things we desire the most. Then, when we get to the years at the end of our lives and look back, we realize the biggest regrets are from not pursuing more of the things we desired the most. How do I know this? Well, I Googled "top regrets of the dying." Here is the resulting list:

They wish they had been more loving to the people who mattered most.

They wish they had been a better spouse, parent, or child.

They wish they had not spent so much time working.

They wish they had taken more risks.

They wish they had been happier and enjoyed life more.

They wish they had lived their dream.

They wish they had taken better care of themselves.

They wish they had done more for others.

They wish they had chosen more meaningful work.

Hmmmm. What's missing from that list? None of them had wished they had avoided fear, failure, or rejection. None wished they had taken fewer risks, *passed* on more adventures, or pursued smaller goals.

One of the greatest self-improvement routines you can have is spending regular time with the elderly. They've been there and done that. They know what worked and what didn't. They don't hold back when it comes to the things they are most proud of and the things they regret. Just ask them.

And by the way, as I typed out this "top regrets of the dying" list, I couldn't help but think about how so many of the essential F-word lessons you are receiving in this book will help you avoid having these regrets at the end of your life. Take a look:

They wish they had been more loving to the people who mattered most—Family and Friends.

They wish they had been a better spouse, parent, or child—Family, Forgiveness and Future You.

They wish they had not spent so much time working—Finances and Foundational Habits.

They wish they had taken more risks—Failure, Faith, Future You and Foundational Habits.

They wish they had been happier and enjoyed life more—all nine apply here.

They wish they had lived their dream—Faith, Future You and Foundational Habits.

They wish they had taken better care of themselves—Fitness and Foundational Habits.

They wish they had done more for others—Forgiveness, Finances, Future You.

They wish they had chosen more meaningful work—Foundational Habits and Future You.

Dr. Kevin Elko shared two simple questions during a seminar I attended years ago, and they changed my life forever.

So what?

Now what?

After every rejection or failure in your life, ask yourself those two magical questions. So what? Now what? This will remind you that you have almost no control over the events that happen to you.

Write down this formula:

$E + R = O$ or Event + Response = Outcome

We just covered the event (E). Again, you have almost no control over the events that happen in your life.

The only thing you can control is your response (R) to each event.

Your response determines the outcome (O).

Create a three-second pause between an event and your response to that event. During those three seconds, ask yourself, "So what? Now what?" This three-second pause and the answer to the question will improve your response and create more favorable outcomes throughout your life.

Unfortunately, bad things happen to good people every day.

You will be rejected.

You will be told no.

You will meet ignorant people who say ignorant things.

You will work your tail off and be told it wasn't enough.

You must understand that you cannot control these events. They aren't your fault.

You *can* control your response. Don't rush it. Respond wisely. The outcome of your life depends on it.

Crossroad:

Throughout your entire life, you will face decisions that offer two basic choices. First, take the path of least resistance, do what's easy or second, take the road less traveled, do what scares you. I'm here to remind you that the easy option will always be available; that's what makes it easy. I'm also here to challenge you to fast forward to your 90th birthday and ask yourself, "Would that version of me be proud of or regret this decision?" That answer will provide your best decision at this crossroad.

3 Things You Need to Know Before Graduation:

- You cannot control the things that happen to you. Trying to do so will only lead to frustration and anger.
- The only thing you have control over in your life is how you choose to respond to each event.
- Saying nothing is always smarter than saying the wrong thing. People can't hear your thoughts. Pause. Take three seconds to give deeper thought to your words before you speak them. Once spoken, there's no going back. A three-second pause between an event and your verbal response better allows you to control the outcome of every situation.

Chapter 4

Own It

"Once you carry your own water,
you will learn the value of every drop."
~Bob Starkey

In chapter one, you learned I wasn't the greatest high school student when it came to taking exams. Now I'm not here to brag, be boastful, or give you my resume, but I am proud of a few things I did manage to accomplish by the time I graduated. One such thing was ranking in the top fifty in my high school class. Granted, I was number forty-nine, and my class only had seventy-one graduates. Yes, I was at the very top of the bottom third! But hey, it was my group of students that actually made the top two-thirds possible!

All kidding aside, school was a struggle for me, as I know it's been for you at times throughout your journey too.

When we struggle or even fail in certain areas, we have a choice. We can point fingers and blame others. We can identify external circumstances that held us back. Or, we can *own our results*. Understand that every result in your life was determined by all of the choices you made leading up to them.

I excelled at picking apart the list of top students in my class and identified all of the reasons I thought they performed better than me. Tara was naturally gifted from kindergarten. Beth didn't play any sports, so she had extra time for schoolwork. Joe's parents were doctors, and they spent a lot of money on tutors for him. The list went on and on. The one thing that was never on my list of reasons why people outperformed me was *me*! I never admitted that my biggest problem was *my* lack of commitment to school. I enjoyed sports, hanging with buddies, spending time with my girlfriend and going to the gym. I chose not to get the grades Tara, Beth, and Joe got. Then, I justified my excuses so I'd feel better about those choices.

So here is my challenge to you in this final chapter of the failure section and every chapter of your life going forward—**own everything in your life, both the good and the bad.**

Don't hide from what's ugly. Don't run away from what was scary. Don't find excuses as to why something didn't turn out as you had hoped. Own it. Own everything.

Also, understand that your past does not determine your future; each present moment does. Yes, I used to be a poor student. Today, I'm a world-class learner. That's a conscious decision that I make each day. You can't change your past, but you should be proud of it. It's all behind you now. Each new day focus on what lies ahead. Your future will be determined by the decisions you make today. Some will be good, others will be bad, but all are yours to take ownership of.

Crossroad:

Your life will be filled with moments where you wish you could have a re-do. You'll speak words you wish you hadn't. You'll act in ways you wish you didn't. Such situations will bring you to this crossroad, and you'll have two choices. You can either lie about it, make excuses, blame somebody or something else, or you can own it. We are all flawed as humans. We all make mistakes. Ask for forgiveness, learn, and move on. Always choose the ownership path.

3 Things You Need to Know Before Graduation:

- Who you were yesterday doesn't determine who you will be tomorrow. Only the decisions you make today will make that determination.
- Your education doesn't end upon your graduation from high school. Challenge yourself to be a lifelong learner. In fact, you need to learn to earn. You may think you aren't smart enough to do something, which may be the case at that very moment, but it doesn't have to be that way forever. Nobody ever knew anything before they did. Give yourself permission to suck at new things. Nobody masters anything immediately.
- Blaming others is simply a ploy to excuse yourself.

Section Summary:

Be proud of your failures. They are proof that you were willing to try. Become a Tribe of Teens member at our website www.tribeofteens.com.

Check out the video online of Tyler and I discussing his thoughts on Failure.

What is one thing you would do if you knew you couldn't fail? Then, do it! Congratulations on completing Section One: Failure. Now you understand there can be no success in the absence of failure.

Section 2

FAITH

Chapter 5
The Lucky Bamboo Tree

"We celebrate people publicly for the work they do in private"
~Tony Robbins

Allow me to introduce you to two teenagers. One is named Eddie Excuses, and the other is Successful Sally. Eddie and Sally typically choose different directions at the crossroads of their lives. For instance, Eddie and Sally once met a multi-millionaire world leader who gave both of them the secret to her success. Simply put, she told them to plant the seeds of a bamboo tree and then continuously water it until it grows. She explained that the only way to fail would be to stop watering those seeds.

On the surface, this seemed easy enough. Both Eddie and Sally planted the bamboo tree seeds, and then each day, they made sure the soil was watered and fertilized morning, afternoon, and night. Day after day, they nurtured the soil and created an ideal growing environment.

After a week, the soil looked exactly the same as it did on day one. In fact, it looked exactly the same after a month. They each thought this was crazy. Every single day, three times a day, they watered this patch of dirt, and absolutely nothing happened. However, they trusted this leader, who shared what she called "life-changing advice with them." Why would she lie?

One month turned into two and two months turned into three. Still nothing. Eddie and Sally's friends would pass by, asking them what they were up to. After explaining they were watering their bamboo trees, their friends laughed. One sarcastically said, "Those aren't trees; they are patches of dirt, no different than three months ago." That friend wasn't wrong.

It was then that Eddie allowed self-doubt to enter his brain.

"What if the seeds I planted were no good?"

"What if the soil is bad?"

"What if the temperatures aren't right?"

"What if this lady was wrong?"

"How many more days am I going to waste time watering and fertilizing this patch of dirt and getting laughed at with no results?"

The answer was zero. Eddie was done wasting his time on this project. He tried, and it didn't work. He had a solid list of excuses for why it was no longer worth his time and effort.

Sally chose to press on. Months turned into a year, and one year turned into two. Two full years of getting up each morning to water a patch of soil with nothing in return, not even a little green sprout. Self-doubt crept into Sally's mind the same way it did with Eddie. Her friends continued laughing at her, and some even questioned her sanity, but she refused to quit. Each time quitting entered her mind, she refocused on the successful world leader who shared stories of how her life and the lives of so many other successful friends had changed forever once their bamboo trees grew. She warned Eddie and Sally that it wouldn't be a quick and easy process, but she encouraged them to have *faith* and promised their efforts would be rewarded. Sally pressed on.

Two years turned into three, and then three years turned into four. Still, no sign of a bamboo tree.

And then it happened. One magical moment while watering her patch of soil for the four thousandth time, a bright green sprout emerged from the earth and grew six inches tall. Sally was elated. Her hard work and perseverance were finally going to pay off. The next morning that sprout grew another two feet, with new sprouts growing from it. The next day the baby bamboo tree was now taller than Sally. And before she knew it, four weeks had passed, and her bamboo tree had grown to over eighty feet tall! It now stood the same height as a four-story building.

Suddenly everything in Sally's life changed just like the world leader had promised her four years earlier. Sally's happiness increased, her wealth expanded, and opportunities became abundant. Her friends started to call this her lucky bamboo tree.

Was it actually *luck*, though? Or was this the result of four years of dedication, focused work, and commitment to a single goal?

And did that tree really grow eighty feet in four weeks? Or did it grow underneath that soil Sally was watering every day for four straight years?

Faith and Grit

The two words you just read above will change the direction of your life forever if you choose.

Faith is the complete trust and belief in something or somebody.

Grit is the dedicated action required to continuously follow your *faith* even though you cannot see the results.

Four years earlier, Eddie and Sally began watering the soil, and they both had faith that a bamboo tree would grow. What they didn't know at the time was from the moment those first drops of water hit their seeds, the tree began to grow underground.

As they continued to water and fertilize the soil, a root system expanded and grew stronger beneath the surface. It was building the rock-solid foundation required to eventually one day explode from the earth and support an eighty-foot tree.

They both started with faith but only maintained the grit required to show up every morning to care for that soil. When Eddie's grit stopped, so too did his faith that something good would happen, and on that day, his lucky bamboo tree died.

Crossroad:

Anything worth having is worth working for. Throughout your life's journey, you will pursue many passions. Along the way, you will arrive at some of the most challenging crossroads. Your option will be to fight through the failures and push through the pain of not realizing results or surrender to that voice in your head telling you to stop. It is my deep, loving wish for you never to surrender. Have faith; work with grit.

3 Things You Need to Know Before Graduation:

- Both positive and negative results are often invisible at first. Everything we choose to do or not to do matters.
- When you truly believe in something or somebody with all of your heart, pursue that passion and protect your strong beliefs from naysayers. Not everyone will see, believe, or understand your vision, and that's okay. In fact, that's what makes it your vision.
- There is no such thing as overnight success. The actress, singer, or athlete that just hit the mainstream and is suddenly making millions of dollars didn't just start putting in the work recently. You just happen to see the results of their work now. They put in years of faith and grit to earn what they are receiving. It wasn't luck. It never is.

Chapter 6
Everything Happens For You

*"I am a great believer in luck,
and the harder I work the more I have of it."*
~Thomas Jefferson

One of my favorite parables is about a farmer with a son and a horse. The story takes place one hundred years ago and goes like this. . .

One day the farmer's only horse ran away.

Quickly his neighbors rushed over to let the farmer know how sorry they were and how *unlucky* he was because this happened.

The farmer responded, "Perhaps," as he shrugged his shoulders.

A few days later, the horse returned, and along with it came three other wild horses. Quickly his neighbors rushed over to rejoice with the farmer. They proclaimed what a great day this was and how *lucky* he was to now have four horses. The farmer responded, "Perhaps," as he shrugged his shoulders.

The following day the farmer's only son tried to ride one of the untamed horses. The horse threw him to the ground, and in doing so, the boy broke his leg. The neighbors rushed over to sympathize with the farmer, and they touted how *unlucky* this situation was. The farmer responded, "Perhaps," as he shrugged his shoulders.

Two days later, members of the army came through town, recruiting young men to fight in the war. Upon arriving at the farmer's house and seeing his son with a broken leg, they passed him by. Once again, the neighbors chimed in, sharing just how *lucky* the farmer was. The farmer responded, "Perhaps," as he shrugged his shoulders.

The point is this, everything that happens in life will happen for you, not to you. Rarely do we recognize that events that seem unfortunate at the time are actually blessings in the long term. You have to have *faith*, no matter what the present moment may look like.

We all experience a *recency bias*. This means we tend to believe that whatever events are happening in our life right now, today, at this very moment—good or bad—will last forever. I'm here to remind you that nothing lasts forever. Good times will turn to bad and bad times will turn to good. Rarely do we understand why at the time. During dark moments, keep the faith that bright days lie ahead, and during happy times, fully embrace that moment because they come in small doses. Stay present and live fully in each short period of time. Understand that everything happens for a reason, and plenty of questions simply have no answers. During times like these, when friends, family, and neighbors rush to remind you how lucky or unlucky you are, take some advice from the farmer and say, "*Perhaps,*" as you shrug your shoulders.

Lucky or Unlucky?

In my senior year of high school, I was one of six football players looking to play at the college level. Two of the six knew exactly where they wanted to attend college. Three other close friends and I visited numerous schools on recruit weekends. After a few months of visits, all four of us decided on the same college. We would all attend together in the fall and continue to play football with one another. The problem was only three of us got accepted to that college. Yup, you guessed it, I was the one who didn't get in. I appealed that decision; I went and interviewed with the college's admission board, and they still said no. I was crushed. I spent the entire summer upset about it. I didn't understand why this was happening to me. I felt it wasn't fair.

Fast forward one year. My three buddies, who went to that desired school together, all flunked out. They were more interested in what that school offered regarding parties than studying and playing ball. I am certain that had I been accepted to that school with them, I, too, would have flunked out alongside them.

Fast forward one more year. I'm now in the fall semester of junior year when a blonde-haired, blue-eyed freshman stepped foot onto the campus at my college. We spent time together, discovered we had a lot in common and decided we'd date one another exclusively at the end of the school year. Yes, that pretty freshman girl is now my wife of twenty-plus years and the mother to my three amazing children.

When I was the only person who didn't get into that college with my buddies, I didn't understand why. My recency bias had me believing my college career would suck forever. What I didn't realize at the time is that *life happens for you, not to you.* After four years, I had a bachelor's degree, discovered a passion for writing, met incredible lifelong friends and bonded with a beautiful soul with whom I will spend the rest of my days.

Crossroad:

You will arrive at many crossroads because things didn't go the way you planned. Unfortunate events will occur, and it will seem like you have no *luck*. At these crossroads, your options are to throw a pity party and feel sorry for yourself, or you can shrug your shoulders, accept the fact that you cannot change what happened, and move forward with the *faith* that whatever is happening is happening for a reason. Ultimately, it's all happening for you.

3 Things You Need to Know Before Graduation:

- When a window closes, a door opens. Changes throughout your career and in your life may seem devastating at the time but often lead to greater opportunities elsewhere.
- Understand that everything happens for a reason, and very rarely, if ever, will you understand that reason in the present moment.
- We all have a recency bias. During a breakup, we think, *I'll never love somebody that much again*, or *I'll never find somebody that good again*. Yes, you will. When we lose a job or money, we think *I'll never find a job that good or have money again*. Yes, you will. Everything in life is temporary. Be patient. The reasons why will show up in the future.

Chapter 7
Let's Get STUPID

"Any fool can condemn, criticize and complain,
and most fools do."
~Dale Carnegie

During my career, I was told that goals should be SMART:

Specific,

Measurable,

Attainable,

Realistic,

Timeline.

I'm not saying it's a bad formula, but I am telling you that it's a boring approach that challenges you to play small. There is a place for SMART goals, but in this chapter, I'm going to challenge you to challenge yourself to dream bigger. So big that people laugh at you, tell you you're crazy and even think to themselves, *That's stupid.* And they'd be right.

However, they wouldn't realize you are following the STUPID acronym:

Scary,

Teachable,

Unbelievable,

Positive,

Impactful,

Dream.

Scary: If something doesn't challenge you, it will never change you. All change is scary. Big changes are especially scary because your likelihood of failure increases. Remember, it's that fear of failure which sits at the core of why we don't pursue bigger dreams. Step one in this process is to set a goal so big that the mere thought of it gives you butterflies.

Teachable: Can you teach yourself or surround yourself with others who can teach you how to make this goal a reality? The answer is YES. Become a knowledge junkie and take every free minute to consume the information you need to accomplish your desired goal. Soon you will learn that it's *WHO*, not *HOW*. Seek out those with similar goals, lofty expectations, and have already been to the places you want to go. Spend more time with those who can teach you.

Unbelievable: If you told a friend in 1869 that we'd put a human being on the moon in 1969, they would never believe it. If you told a caveman dependent on fire that one day we'd flip a switch and light an entire room, he'd never believe you. If you told me when I was in grade school that I could type a few words onto a computer and instantly have endless information on that subject—thanks, Google—I'd never believe you. My point is nothing was ever believable before it became a reality. Is your goal something that nine out of ten people wouldn't believe is possible? If so, you're on the right track!

Positive and Impactful: I will cover these together. Will your goal make a positive impact on the world? Is it a solution to a problem? Who will it serve? How will it make their lives better? How long will people remember you and your life's work? It has been said that, as humans, we all have *two* death dates. The first is the day we physically die, and the second is the day the last person who speaks our name dies.

That's deep; take a second to re-read that sentence.

Our legacy continues after our physical death as long as people continue to remember our work and speak our name. Will your STUPID goal make such a long-lasting, positive impact that people will still be speaking your name one hundred years after you take your last breath? It absolutely can, and I believe it will!

Dream: If something is in your head, it's a dream. If you write that dream on paper, it's a goal. If you verbalize that goal to the world, now it's a commitment. My challenge to you is to take your STUPID goal and write it down, then share it with the world. Sure, people will laugh at you. The masses laugh at every idea that doesn't fit inside society's normal, boring box. Now I want you to become obsessed with your STUPID goal. When you wake up in the morning, I want you to spend your first sixty seconds visualizing it as if you've already made it a reality. Before you go to bed at night, I want you to visualize it as if you've already made it a reality. During the day, I want you to speak your goal to the universe aloud—I do this in the shower each morning.

In the next chapter, I will walk you through creating a vision board so you can see what this goal will look like. Your *obsessions will become your possessions* in life. Whatever you constantly think about and ask for will be what your brain searches for. The thoughts you have in your head will become what you have in your life. Dream big, allow these STUPID thoughts in your head, share your intentions with the world, and you'll live the life you desire.

Crossroad:

You are growing up during a time when the masses encourage you to play the game of life small. You will encounter BIG opportunities that will seem silly to people who don't dream as grand as you do. When you approach these crossroads, you'll have a choice to make. Do you listen to the masses and play it safe, remain average and be comfortable? Or, do you take a chance, follow your dreams, and welcome the potential failure and laughter that may follow? Just remember this, *nobody ever accomplished anything amazing in life because of everything they were going to do.* Dream BIG, and never stop believing you can have anything you desire.

3 Things You Need to Know Before Graduation:

- While the safe road is comfortable, it's lined with stories of people with unlimited potential and minimal results who listened to the masses. You are young; you have time on your side. Don't be afraid to take chances now. You will learn from failures and adjust as needed.
- It only takes one great idea to change your life and potentially impact millions. Don't allow one failure to stop your pursuit of your ONE great idea.
- Think of the world as a cave. When you scream a word into a cave, the cave echoes that word back to you. Whatever you give, you get back. Take all of your amazing, positive thoughts and big dreams to *life's cave* and scream them out. The universe will send more of the same right back to you.

Chapter 8
Vision Board

"Be brave enough to live the life of your dreams according to your vision and purpose instead of the expectations and opinions of others."
~Roy T Bennett

When you reflect on your school career, if you're anything like me, some of your favorite moments came during recreation time—arts and crafts, playing during recess, coloring, or any other activity which allowed you to get creative and be your true self.

To put a bow on this **FAITH** section, I'm going to encourage you to get creative and even a bit *crafty*. I want you to create a vision board. Pause here, close your eyes and *picture, in great detail, what you believe to be your perfect future life.*

VISION IN PROGRESS

Welcome back! I specifically didn't give you detailed instructions for that exercise because I didn't want to steer your vision. After all, it's *yours*, not mine. Your vision may have been short or long-term in nature. It may have been things you can accomplish this year or things that could take a lifetime. Understand that your vision will change throughout your life. There will never be one final destination. Too often, people tell themselves things like, *Once I have this type of home, drive this type of car, have this much money in my bank account. . . then, I will be fulfilled and happy.*

Guess what happens next? They buy that house, drive that car, and have that money and discover they still aren't fulfilled and happy. Why not? Because their vision didn't evolve and expand as their journey through life did. I'm not saying to exclude materialistic things on your vision board—again, it's your vision, not mine. However, I am reminding you that your vision today may not be your vision a year from now, and that's okay. Once created, you will obsess over what you see on that board daily. You will keep it visible so you can visit it multiple times daily. And if there is ever a moment when something on that board no longer aligns with your values, beliefs, passion, and purpose. . . update your board!

For years my board was filled with materialistic visions. Today, it still has a picture of the home on the lake that I will someday own. However, I've shifted from wanting to earn a million dollars each year to now wanting to donate a million dollars each year. In fact, writing this book has been on my board for years, and its resulting effect will help me take one step closer to my charitable goals as well. It takes time, but ultimately everything you have on your vision board will begin to work together to help you realize your life's vision and purpose.

Let's start at the very beginning first. Everybody learns differently, has different styles, and uniquely processes information. Determine what works best for you. Do you like paper pictures? Do you prefer digital? Do you enjoy writing and reading written words? Or is it a combination of everything? There's no wrong answer here; pick the style you prefer.

Next, go back to your visions earlier in this chapter when I encouraged you to pause and picture your best life. What did you see? Take those images and make them real. Write them on paper. And finally, create your board using those visions. Again, this could be cutting out, printing, or drawing pictures. It could be on a big or small poster board. It could be digital, handwritten or a combination of all. Whatever works for you, make it happen. In fact, do it now. Take a few moments to transfer your vision from your head onto paper by writing down, in great detail, everything you see in your future.

VISION TRANSFER IN PROGRESS

Congratulations! You just took the first GIANT step toward making your vision a reality. You've heard me reference "the masses" and taking a "contrarian approach" to what the masses are doing. Well, by completing your vision board, you did just that! Nine out of ten humans on the planet have never moved the visions from their brains onto paper. You are now in an elite minority of people committed to making things happen.

Now for the hard part—commit to this exercise long-term.

Spend sixty seconds thinking about this vision as if it's already a reality each morning.

Spend sixty seconds thinking about this vision as if it's already a reality each evening.

Physically look at this vision throughout the day, every day.

Adjust your vision as your life evolves.

Be patient. Everything worth having in this world is worth working for and waiting for. Everything you want will happen, but it won't happen overnight or without relentless focus.

Crossroad:

You will encounter numerous moments where you reflect and realize that everything in your current reality seems to be completely opposite of what you see on your vision board. You can throw your vision away, or you can keep the *faith*. Of all the essential F-words we cover in this book, *faith* might be the most important. It's also the most difficult to stick with because you cannot see all of the invisible magic happening.

3 Things You Need to Know Before Graduation:

- You have the ability to write your own book. You determine your future chapters today; just spell out the specific details you desire.
- People want everything immediately. Those who receive everything they want are those who patiently continue to put in the work despite the fact they do not see immediate results.
- Faith is the deep belief you have in something or somebody. You must have faith in yourself, knowing that the things you are telling yourself—your personal affirmations, you already are. And the things you focus on—your vision board, you will

become. Faith gives you the ability to stick with invisible progress consistently.

Section Summary

You are that Chinese bamboo tree. Your vision board and commitment to continuous improvement create a robust root system below the surface. Your faith and belief that everything on that board WILL become a reality are the water and nourishment required to one day allow everything you desire to explode from the earth. But you cannot quit, and you can never stop believing. Always keep the faith. *Never quit on the grit* required to get to where you want to be.

Also, when you initially saw this section was about faith, chances are your mind immediately went to religious faith. While I am a man of deep religious faith, I intentionally did not go down that road in this section. I made this choice out of respect for every reader's unique and personal beliefs. If you have religious faith, that is awesome; never let that go. A deep belief in whichever higher power you believe in will guide you and pull you through the most difficult times in your life. Remember, by definition, faith is *complete trust or confidence in someone or something*. That's an amazing thing to have, regardless of who your someone or something is!

Check out the video online of Tyler and I discussing his thoughts on Faith at www.tribeofteens.com

Section 3

Foundational Habits

Chapter 9
Get the Little Things Right

"If you cannot do great things, do small things in a great way."
~Napolean Hill

In 1962, President John F. Kennedy visited NASA for the first time. During the facility tour, while walking down a hallway, Kennedy and his team passed a custodian pushing a broom. The President stopped and introduced himself to this man. After asking for his name and a few other simple questions, the President asked the custodian what he did for NASA. Without hesitation, the man proudly replied, "I'm helping put a man on the moon."

Please pause and reflect on what happened there. The custodian understood something that most people struggle with, *his work was significant, and he mattered.* Keeping that building clean allowed scientists and astronauts to focus on the overall mission of putting a man on the moon. Nobody in that building had to stress about who would take out the trash or clean the bathrooms because the custodian had their backs in that department. He understood how his role was significant to the overall mission of NASA and was able to play a part in the organization's success.

Too often, we believe that the little things simply do not matter. But how can anyone accomplish big goals when they aren't willing to get the little things right first?

Hang the Towel

Life is filled with things you cannot control. You must focus on controlling the things you can. For instance, remember that towel you threw on the floor instead of hanging it up where it belonged? In the big scheme of things, no big deal, right?

Would taking an extra second to hang that towel versus throwing it on the floor change your life forever?

Probably not.

However, it creates the framework for long-term success habits. No change happens from a singular event. The intentional focus on doing the little things consistently will compound over time, allowing you to reach your full potential.

Hang the Towel: This simple act will reinforce that you are the person who does things the right way. You are not lazy and do not expect others to do things for you that you can do yourself.

Make Your Bed: It's essential to build momentum within each of your days. The easiest way to do this is by accomplishing something early in your day. As soon as you get up, take five minutes to make your bed. Before leaving your bedroom, check out that neat-looking bed and be proud of your work. Then, move on to your next small win.

Put Things Back: Keep yourself organized, and save time and stress in the future by simply putting things back where they belong when you are done with them. You'll never have a big cleanup project when you take care of things as you go. Also, when you have a mess or clutter and cannot find things you need when you need them, your stress levels will increase, and you'll become less productive.

Pick Up the Trash, Even if It's Not Yours: This one isn't easy because you didn't do it! However, if everyone took a second to pick up something they saw that shouldn't be there, the world would be a clean. If you are serious about wanting to make the world a better place, take a second to pick something up rather than just walk by.

Express Gratitude. *You can't be hateful when you're grateful* and when you have an attitude of gratitude, you'll attract the right type of people into your life. Be thankful for everything in your life, the good and the bad. Remember, **everything is happening for you, not to you. . .** even when you don't understand why.

Say Something Nice When it's Least Expected: You can seek blessings from others, or you can work to be a blessing to others. Find at least one opportunity each day to say, write, or text something nice and unexpected to somebody else.

Show Up Early: Time is our most precious asset. The wealthiest eighty-five-year-old in the world would trade all of their wealth to return to being a fifteen-year-old again. Why? Because you can always make money, but you cannot use it to buy back time. So, what does this have to do with showing up early? It's outrageously disrespectful to waste another human's time. Also, when you show up late, you silently tell other people that your time is more precious than theirs. When others show up on time and you don't, it sends all of the wrong signals.

Floss Your Teeth: You only get one set of teeth and gums; take care of them. Live life with attention to detail with everything. Taking just sixty seconds each day to floss your teeth will reduce your chances of tooth decay, cavities, and gum disease. There is also a connection between flossing and improved heart health. Studies show that people who floss daily live over six years longer than those who do not. And finally, taking care of your teeth and flossing will give you better breath, and who wants to be around people with horrific breath? Take care of your teeth, floss daily, let your big smile shine, and talk to people with sparkling confidence.

Exercise One Extra Minute: Simple math. . . one extra minute each day is seven minutes a week, and 364 minutes a year. That's six additional hours. If you exercise for thirty minutes each day, bumping that up *to thirty-one* minutes will add twelve extra thirty-minute workouts to your year! Those who accomplish big things do the little things, even if it's just for one minute.

It's these little things that will make you a bigger person—a better version of yourself. The quality of your life will be determined by the sum of each small decision you choose to make as well as those you choose *not* to make.

What if that custodian didn't consistently take out the trash, sweep the floors, and keep the bathrooms sparkling clean at NASA? Is it possible that the scientists, engineers, and astronauts would become upset and annoyed? And would that negative energy limit their capacity to dream bigger, more innovative ideas? And if those ideas were blocked, would we have put a man on the moon? Maybe. Maybe not. That custodian was a big part of the NASA team. Most would overlook his role because he only did the little things. However, it's all of those things that make the *biggest* difference.

In the next two chapters, I share systems, processes and habits that will positively change your life forever. As you read about them, you'll notice they are all pretty easy to do. However, they will also seem like little things, which won't matter if you skip them. The difference between flying among the stars and being stuck on the ground is the consistent execution of the little things.

Crossroad:

Any time you are faced with a choice to do something now or take care of it later, choose the "do it now road." By letting things linger, they weigh on you as they sit on your to-do list. This adds to your stress levels and holds you back from the most productive, happiest version of yourself. And, oftentimes, the things you say you will do later never actually get done.

3 Things You Need to Know Before Graduation:

- The daily tasks that don't seem like a big deal are the biggest deals of all.
- Your choices around doing or not doing the little things send a message to your brain which validates the type of person you are.
- Momentum is a powerful force you can harness by accomplishing simple tasks as soon as you wake up.

Chapter 10
Morning Routine

"If you win the morning, you win the day."
~Tim Ferris

I'm going to kick this chapter off with an obvious but difficult part of having a morning routine—waking up. I'm not going to give you a specific time to wake up because everyone is different, and throughout your life, your work schedule may change. So rather than saying you should wake up at this specific time, my challenge to you is to determine what time you need to start your day, then wake up thirty minutes earlier. And now, for the part of the book that may cause you to think I'm absolutely insane. . . when your alarm goes off, don't hit snooze; just get up.

Yes, I realize asking a teenager to consider waking up thirty minutes earlier and to skip hitting the snooze button is a radical idea. However, keep in mind that every word written in this book is designed to improve your life and to share with you the *cheat code* from some of the most successful adults I've worked with in the corporate world. They understand that to win their day; they must win their mornings. The decision to own those thirty minutes in the morning and become intentional with that time moves you from being average to elite. Remember, every decision you make matters, and the first decision of your day will always be, "Do I wake up and attack this day? Or do I go back to bed while other people are up attacking theirs?" Your values and the person you become in life will be determined by the number of promises you keep to yourself. Setting an alarm clock is a promise. Your feet on the floor when it wakes you is the keeping of that promise. Start each day with a mindset of attack, not react.

*Now, if you currently have a relationship with your snooze button that you can't just break immediately, here's an alternative solution. Instead of setting that alarm for thirty minutes earlier, set it for forty minutes. Problem solved. You can now hit that snooze button once and use those ten minutes to ease into your day. However, you must protect your first thirty minutes because once the six daily disciplines I'm about to share with you become **foundational habits**, your life will change forever.*

These six daily disciplines are all things you *can* do. The only reason you won't do them is that you choose not to. Keep in mind you are always striving for *improvement*, not *perfection*. Some days will be better than others with these six disciplines, and that's okay. Also, remember the story of the Chinese bamboo tree. These daily disciplines represent continuously watering the soil even though nothing appears to be happening above the surface. I promise you that incorporating these six daily disciplines into your morning routine will create a strong root system, and when your bamboo tree breaks through, it will be an amazing sight to see. Just have **faith** and give it time.

Hydration: You would think that sleeping doesn't take much work. However, your body is still active while you are off dreaming at night. When you wake up, you are dehydrated. As you yawn and your eyes are still only half open, head directly to the kitchen to grab water. As a general rule of thumb, consistently drink half of your body weight in ounces of water each day. If you weigh 160 pounds, you'll want to consume eighty ounces of water. Start this process ASAP. Chug down as much as you can as soon as you wake up. This will help energize your body.

Meditation: As if I didn't already ask for enough with skipping the snooze button, now I am going to throw meditation at you in this chapter too? Yup! I know what you immediately think when I mention meditation. You picture a monk, wearing a silk robe, sitting cross-legged on top of a mountain with his palms to the sky as incense is burning and spiritual music is playing. You're also thinking, *There's no way I'm doing that!* Stick with me on this one. The reason I am asking you to spend at least five minutes at the start of each day practicing meditation is because I truly believe it's the most important five minutes of your day.

Let's begin with a misconception. Most people believe meditation is a person closing their eyes and eliminating all thoughts from their head. And as soon as a thought enters their brain, they lose, and the meditation session is over. It's actually just the opposite. Meditation is all about learning to be where your feet are. What does that mean? Being present and living within each moment throughout your day. Today, more than ever, you are living in a fast-paced, instant-answer, immediate gratification world filled with technological stimulations and digital distractions.

How do you quiet all of it? How do you ignore the endless electronic algorithms and people who pull your attention in a thousand different directions? It's a skill. And this skill is learned and developed in meditation sessions each morning. Simply put, you will have random thoughts that pop into your mind during your meditation practice. It's natural. The goal is to be aware of the thought and recognize it doesn't belong there at the moment. So, recognize it, move it out of your head and then come back to focusing on your breathing. When you do this consistently, you're training your brain over time to eliminate random thoughts and distractions that pop into your brain throughout the day. By remaining focused and present within each moment, you'll become more efficient with your time, less stressed, and ultra-productive.

I've spent the past twenty years studying the foundational habits of millionaires, billionaires, thought leaders and the happiest, healthiest people on the planet. These people have many **foundational habits** in common; meditation stands out the most. Almost every person within these groups has a meditation practice as part of their daily routines.

And finally, you can use digital technology to help you with this practice. Apps from Calm, Head Space, Peloton, and others offer various types and lengths of guided meditations. Just hit play and follow along!

Positive Journaling: For the next five minutes of your day, jot down every single positive thing that comes to your mind from yesterday. The world sends us a disproportionate number of negative to positive stories. To make things worse, our brains seek negativity as a survival mechanism—they are on high alert to find danger to keep us safe. Once you understand this, you'll begin to find opportunities to seek joy. They are typically found in the most simplistic moments. The daily act of positive journaling will allow you to recall all of the good things that happen throughout your day, and there are plenty. The magic of this exercise is when your brain knows it will be asked to recall these positive moments first thing each morning, it then spends the day scanning the world for *more positives* and finds them. What a blessing, right? How amazing life becomes when you constantly see all of the good that surrounds you. This daily practice will make you happier and healthier.

Here is a pro tip from somebody who has been doing this for years, *don't overthink things*. Too often, we tend to look for huge moments to add to our lists. However, the reality is huge moments rarely happen and certainly don't happen daily. Instead, look for the *little things.* Any moments that make you smile or you find small pleasures in, jot those down. After all, this is your list, so there are no wrong answers. Perhaps you see a blue jay in a tree. Maybe you opened a new jar of peanut butter and took that first spoonful. What about putting that t-shirt on straight from the dryer while it was still warm? Or, you bumped into a friend you haven't seen in a while. These little moments happen daily, and most people forget about them. The act of positive journaling will allow you to relive them the next morning, so you get twice as much joy from the experience.

Also, when you are having a few rough days in a row when nothing seems to be going right, your positive journal can be the best medicine for you. Essentially you're creating a highlight reel. It's awesome to read through all of the positive moments from the prior days, weeks, and months to remind yourself just how amazing you are and your life truly is.

Acts of Kindness: To feel good about yourself, consistently put a smile on the face of another human. Spend the next five-minute block of your morning planning one or two things you can do to make someone else happy. For years people have talked about random acts of kindness. I prefer to replace random—which represents something you cannot control—with *intentional,* something you can control. Everything in this book challenges you to become *intentionally awesome* at the numerous crossroads you encounter. Bringing a smile to somebody's face is no different. Is it a text, e-mail, phone call, handwritten card, or spontaneous visit? Is it a thoughtful gift? Or, is it finding an opportunity to do something small for an unexpecting person? You decide. Use these five minutes of your morning to create a plan to bring joy to somebody's life. The more kindness you give, the more happiness you will have.

The last two daily disciplines can be combined or done separately.

Learn Something: If you enjoy learning by reading, spend five minutes reading a book, blog, or article that will improve you. If you prefer to learn by listening, spend five minutes with a podcast or audio book. Notice the compound effect.

Starting each day with just five minutes of knowledge becomes 1,825 minutes after a year or thirty hours of lessons. Thirty hours is almost an entire work-week. Some people pay $10,000 or more to attend a week-long seminar learning from some of the most brilliant minds on the planet. You live during such an amazing time because you can often consume the same content for free, and you don't even have to leave your house!

Just five minutes each day with some of the most brilliant minds on the planet will yield you the same knowledge you would consume during a week-long seminar each year. At the end of this book, I provide a list of books that profoundly influenced me. I encourage you to read each of them, spending five minutes each morning with one of them over time. Or, review five minutes of this book each morning. Different thoughts and mindsets will hit you at different times throughout your life, so don't just read these words once, make it a practice to review them consistently.

Movement: I spend considerable time on this subject during the Fitness section of the essential F-Words, so I won't dive too deep here. I will remind you that keeping your body stationary without movement is one of the worst things you can do. Knowing this and knowing that you just slept for the past seven hours or so, it's crucial to get your body moving in the morning. You may find that mornings are when you enjoy getting your full-blown daily workouts in, and that's great! However, if that's not the case, then at a minimum, you'll want to spend at least ten minutes moving and stretching your body. This could be sit-ups, pushups, planks, basic weight lifting, stretching, yoga, or whatever else works for you. The key is to do it. Also, if you have a job that has you sitting for hours at a time throughout the day, make sure you are getting yourself up and moving every twenty to thirty minutes. Remember how I talked about water consumption in our first daily discipline? Getting up to consume water every twenty to thirty minutes will not only help you move while getting the water, but it will remind you to get up and move again when you need to release that water!

The 6 Daily Disciplines:

1. Hydration
2. Meditation—5 minutes
3. Positive Journaling—5 minutes
4. Acts of Kindness—5 minutes
5. Learning—5 minutes*
6. Physical Movement—10 minutes*

*indicates can be combined

Crossroad:

You'll arrive at this crossroad 365 times each year, 366 on leap years. When you hear the alarm clock, chances are you won't want to jump right out of bed and dive into these disciplines. The difficult choice will never be easy, but the easy choice will create future difficulties. Once again, the goal is never perfection; instead, it's improvement. You won't always accomplish all six of these daily disciplines. Some days you won't accomplish any. The challenge here is to focus on all six and do your best to check as many boxes as possible. A realistic goal would be fifteen days each month in the beginning. Essentially if you can succeed with all six, just half of the month, that's a tremendous win from the start.

3 Things You Need to Know Before Graduation:

- Living an intentionally awesome life starts by becoming awesomely intentional with your morning actions and activities.
- Build the day's momentum by completing simple tasks which allow you to stack wins and build confidence heading into whatever bigger tasks come next.
- Early risers get a head start in life. They accomplish goals, create plans, and build long-term foundational success habits while others sleep.

Chapter 11
Evening Routine

"You don't decide your future; you decide your habits and your habits decide your future."
~Dr. Mike Murdock

L et's race!

How about a three-mile run? First to the finish line wins. However, not everyone in this race will share the same starting line. Those who choose to sleep in will start their race *three miles* away from the finish line. Those who wake up thirty minutes early and execute their six daily disciplines will start *two miles* away from the finish line. Those who spend thirty minutes before bedtime prepping for sleep and the following day will only have to run *one mile*.

Who do you think has the best opportunity to win this three-mile race? The person who has to run the full three miles, the person who has to run two miles, or the person who only has to run one mile?

I'm guessing your money would be on the person who has to run the shortest distance, right? If so, my challenge to you in this chapter is to be the person with the one-mile race.

Having a solid evening routine will set you up for success in the morning and give you a head start on your competition.

Create a Morning Plan in Advance

Let's craft your evening routine now. The first thing to do is eliminate all unnecessary morning decisions by making those choices the night before. What will you eat for breakfast—can you do anything to prep it in advance? Plan on working out—choose your clothes and lay them out. How about the clothes you'll wear to school or work—select that outfit too. What are your lunch plans—can you prep and pack that in advance? What are your goals for tomorrow, and what's the best first action you need to take to begin working towards them? Write those down.

You get the point. By the time most people have hit their snooze button for the sixth time and finally drag themselves out of bed with no plan for their day, you're already dominating yours. In fact, while they are trying to find their starting line, you are already less than a mile from your finish line.

Our brains only have approximately 600 to 800 calories to burn each day. No different than gas in your car, you have to conserve fuel. You have to be selective with what you spend your energy on, and you can't afford to take too many wrong turns. In the morning, you'll be rested, energized, and have a full tank. This is when you'll want to be creative and do your most crucial activities.

In the evening, your tank is empty. Use this time to make simple, mundane decisions so you aren't wasting your precious morning calories on them.

You should be able to whip through your basic morning decisions in the evening during a ten- to fifteen-minute window. After completing that, it's time to prep for sleep.

Preparing to Sleep

Yes, sleep is something that ultra-productive people prepare for.

Here are a few basic steps.

For starters, do not eat or drink within one hour of your bedtime. As important as hydration is during the day, it's not a good idea in the evening. The goal is to get six to seven hours of quality, uninterrupted sleep. Waking up to use the bathroom will derail that plan.

Having said that, consider drinking a cup of tea before bed. When I read *The 4-Hour Work Week* by Tim Ferris, I was introduced to Yogi Soothing Caramel Bedtime tea, and it changed my sleep forever.

Use your bed for sleeping. Period. Using your bed as a sofa sends your body mixed signals when it's time for sleep.

And now for the big one—and I know it's the one you don't want to hear—avoid electronics, including TV, thirty minutes before your bedtime. Think of how we put babies to sleep. We use lullabies, rocking, and bedtime stories, not TikTok videos. Screen time, whether it's a phone, iPad, computer, or TV, will stimulate your brain, which makes it more difficult to shut down for sleep. A more active brain will also increase the likelihood you'll have dreams, and dreams will prevent you from sleeping as deeply as desired.

Instead of electronics, grab a book to read before bed. Also, consider purchasing a white noise sleep machine to use instead of a television for background noise. As you lie in bed, focus on the quality of your final thoughts for the day. Count your blessings, not your problems or worries. What are you grateful for? Allow positive thoughts to occupy your head before bed!

Bookend your days with strong morning and evening routines. Eliminate unnecessary decisions in the morning by making them at night. Focus on more quality sleep. Wake up thirty minutes earlier than you normally would and immediately execute the six daily disciplines. By becoming strategic with these two thirty-minute time blocks and wildly intentional with the actions and activities within them, you will set yourself up for major daily success. And in the big scheme of things, it's only *one hour* of the twenty-four you receive each day.

Crossroad:

Doing things tomorrow will always be the easy option. And more often than not, you'll want to defer doing things. Especially things that are easy to do later. However, if you haven't learned by now, each crossroad essentially boils down to doing what's easy or choosing the path to exceptional. However, you can't travel down both roads at the same time.

You are going to have tough days. You'll get to the end of those days and want to rest. And I'm not saying you shouldn't do that once in a while, but when you consistently choose that path, you'll eventually wake up in a place you don't want to be. It's then that you'll hire a coach or consultant or decide to read a book to get yourself back on track, and guess what they'll all say?

Get back to the basics.

Own the time that you can.

Have a morning and evening routine.

These are foundational habits you can establish in your teens or foundational habits you can work to rebuild later in your life. My challenge to you is. . . do it now!

<u>3 Things You Need to Know Before Graduation:</u>

- The greatest shortcut you can take is starting your tomorrow the night before.
- Sleep shouldn't be trusted to luck. Make intentional decisions thirty minutes before bed to set yourself up for success in the morning.
- Mornings are easier when all non-essential decisions are decided in advance.

Chapter 12

Stack Winning Days

"Small, seemingly insignificant steps completed consistently over time will create a radical difference."
~Darren Hardy

An upcoming essential F-word is **Finances.** Once we arrive at that chapter, we'll discuss a mountain you will climb when it comes to compounding interest and building significant wealth with time on your side.

The taller the mountain, the greater distance your *investment snow-ball* will travel, picking up speed and growing larger. Building significant wealth becomes easier when you start in your teens.

Knowing you have such an incredible financial opportunity in front of you is fun, right?

Well, now I'm going to show you the other side of that mountain. Because when it comes to establishing long-term foundational success habits, you don't get to take the ski lift to the top. Nope, you have to take the stairs. One-knee-deep snow, burning leg lift at a time. Step. . . after step. . . after painful step.

Just like retirement seems a million miles away, so do all of your big, juicy, scary, hairy, audacious goals. So, in this chapter, my challenge to you is to have lofty goals but not focus on them. Instead, focus on the only thing you can control. . . today. You only get one shot at today. This specific day of the week, date of the month and month of the year is the only such day you'll ever get. And, the likelihood of you accomplishing the small, bite-sized daily goal you set for yourself today is far greater than knocking out your big scary, hairy long-term goals. Set yourself up for success by clearly defining what a winning day looks like today.

One major theme that consistently shows up in this book is *compounding results*. In fact, if compounding started with an "F," it would certainly be one of the most *Essential F-Words for Teens.* All of your results, good and bad, are simply a compounded total of the *small* choices you make.

Your success—however you define it, in life will be determined by the number of winning days you can consistently stack. If you win today, tomorrow, and the day after that, chances are you will win your week. After stacking a few winning weeks, you will have won your month. After stacking winning months, you'll have won your year;

before you know it, all of your winning years will lead you exactly to wherever you want to be. However, none of that can happen if you don't win *today* first.

If I were on my deathbed, with sixty seconds left to live, and you, my first child, sat by my side and asked, "Dad, what's just one thing I can do to live my best life?"

"Winning days" would be my answer.

Peter Drucker was known as one of the greatest minds in the field of business management. He once stated, "There is nothing so useless as doing efficiently that which should not be done at all." Those words deeply resonated with me and forced me to take a daily inventory of the things I was spending my time doing. I share Peter's words with you so you can clearly define what a winning day looks like in your world each morning. This practice will allow you to then focus your energy on the most essential tasks and activities that will get you there.

Only concentrate on the one thing you can control, this present day. Be where your feet are. Be present. Have faith and follow your daily routines. Clearly define a few actions and activities you need to accomplish today, and everything beyond that will take care of itself. All of the stress and uncertainty of what could happen today, as well as the fear and anxiety of what has happened in the past, make zero difference. The only thing that matters is being the best version of you today. *Just win your day.*

Ups and Downs

We love rollercoasters. Perhaps it's the uncertainty of what is going to happen. Perhaps it's our willingness to let go of all control and just go where the next two minutes will take us. Perhaps it's the commitment to not turning back. Once we are locked in and that machine steamrolls forward, we are all in. There's no getting off.

Well, life is a rollercoaster. But for some reason, we find the *thrills* and *surprises* less exciting. There will be climbs; there will be parts that you find exhilarating and moments when you're left breathless. You may scream and cry, but when that machine screeches to a halt, you're never upset that you locked yourself into it.

Some days you'll win. Some days you'll lose. That's just how it goes. For your own safety and mental stability, I'd encourage you not to look much deeper than that.

The secret is to ride the highs for as long as you can and fight through the lows as fast as you can. But understand that both are temporary. They are intertwined, and one always leads to the other. That's just how the rollercoaster of life works. You'll have ups and downs, highs and lows, but ultimately you only control the moments within your present day. Clearly identify what each winning day looks like and keep your energy focused there. The more winning days you stack up, the more you'll enjoy your ride!

Crossroad:

Often people don't like to keep score because they are scared of losing. The simple solution to eliminate that fear is to eliminate the scoreboard. When you have such thoughts, you are at another crossroads. Do I keep track of and score my food choices? My fitness choices? My evening and morning routines? The execution of my six daily disciplines? What my winning day looks like? Choosing not to keep score is easy. It also eliminates your ability to celebrate success and improve upon failures. Life already keeps score for you, so you might as well make that scoreboard visible each day.

3 Things You Need to Know Before Graduation:

- Long-term success happens one winning day at a time.
- Expect highs and lows in life. Ride the highs as long as possible and understand that the lows are only temporary.
- Be present in each moment. You can't change the past, and you can't control the future. All you'll ever own in life is the right now. Don't miss it!

Section Summary

Remember the story of the three little pigs and the big, bad wolf? Each of the little pigs chose to build their homes with different materials. The first chose straw, the second chose sticks, and the third chose bricks. The big, bad wolf visited each home, and he huffed and puffed and tried to blow each house down. He was successful with two out of three. The brick home stood strong.

Your foundational habits are the bricks you'll use to build a strong life. The big, bad wolf is life itself. From time to time, it will huff and puff and attempt to blow your house down. The thicker your bricks, the stronger you'll stand!

As a Tribe of Teens member, you get to hear Tyler's take on foundational habits. Check it out at www.tribeofteens.com.

CONGRATULATIONS!!!!

You are now one-third of the way through the nine *Essential F-Words for Teens!*

33.33333333333333% progress is no small feat.

Stand up, stretch out, and pat yourself on the back.

You now know the truth about **FAILURE**—it's NOT a bad thing.

You understand the importance of **FAITH**—believing good things will happen even when you don't know how, when, or why.

You are building **FOUNDATIONAL HABITS**—taking control of what you can control and consistently getting the little things right.

Deep breath…

Now let's dive into the next three sections:

FRIENDS, FAMILY and FORGIVENESS

Section 4
FRIENDS

Chapter 13

It's Who, Not How

"I don't need to know everything. I just need to know where to find it when I need it."
~Henry Ford

Your entire life, you've searched for the way to do things. While in diapers, you decided one day to make a bold move and attempted to crawl. Your arms gave out, and you fell on your face. Eventually, you did figure it out.

After you got sick of crawling, you pulled yourself up alongside the couch and practiced "surfing" as you shuffled side to side while hanging onto the cushions for dear life! This led to the brave attempt to walk. Your legs gave out a few times, causing you to fall on your face. Eventually, you did figure it out.

When you started pre-kindergarten class, you dealt with major separation anxiety as it was the first time you spent significant hours without family nearby. You found a buddy to walk the hallway with each morning, and eventually, you did figure it out.

Attempting to read the words in a book. How do they sound? What do they mean? Initially, you had no clue. You stuttered, stammered, and got a few confused along the way, but eventually, you did figure it out.

In each of these situations and scenarios, you were never alone. As your initial crawling and first-step adventures were happening, Mom and I were there to pick you up. When you freaked out about being left alone at school, your buddy, Michael, guided you down the hallway and into the classroom. When you initially struggled with reading, your teachers were patient and supportive until you learned the words and their meanings.

One of the most beautiful things about life is that you rarely have to do anything alone. Friendly faces are always nearby to help you. So, ask the question, take the leap, celebrate your wins, and surround yourself with good friends. We spend too much of our time and energy seeking to answer the question, "How do I do this?" Instead, we need to ask ourselves, "Who should I do this with?" Or, "Who has already done this before."

Jim Rohn once said, "You are the average of the five people you spend the most time with." In fact, I believe the greatest predictor of who you will become in the future is the people you are choosing to spend time with in the present.

I wasn't much older than you are now when I met one of my first mentors in the field of sales. His name was Lou. Lou was one of my mother's friends who had recruited me into a multi-line-home-based business. He asked me to schedule ten meetings with people so he could present our products and business opportunity. He would demonstrate the art of sales so I could learn from him and ultimately do it on my own. I called every one of my friends, and after a few days, I had ten appointments scheduled. Lou and I met with each of them, and when all of the meetings were over, we had a total of zero sales. Nothing, nada, zip, zilch, zero. Lou then gave me some advice that changed my life forever. He said, "Scott, if you want to succeed in business or any other area of life, you have to surround yourself with people who have already done whatever it is you want to do."

If I'm being honest, those words didn't make much sense to me at the time. It wasn't until a few weeks later that I realized I was asking people my age, teenagers, to consider investing in a business opportunity that simply didn't make sense to them at that point in their life. Most had no money, were still living at home, had no business experience, and were more concerned about finding fake IDs and getting into bars than they were about building a strong financial future. Lou challenged me to talk to people with a different vision. He asked me who the doctors, lawyers, small business owners, teachers and other experienced leaders in the community were. He challenged me to call and schedule appointments with them. I made a list of those people and quickly became scared to death to make calls because I assumed they wouldn't listen to a know-nothing kid asking them to explore a home-based business opportunity. Clearly, I didn't have access to the "Failure" section of this book at the time. Quickly I realized I was wrong.

While I may have been a know-nothing kid, Lou wasn't. Lou was experienced and masterful at sales; he was everything I wanted to become. He wore nice clothes, picked up the tab at every lunch and drove a Mercedes. Once I started scheduling appointments for community leaders to meet with Lou, my sales results exploded. I learned that initially, I was spending too much time trying to figure out how to sell. Once I discovered who to schedule appointments with and who I needed to meet with, my world changed.

Focus on who you surround yourself with in life and less on *how* to do things. It worked when you learned to crawl, walk, go to school, and read. I promise you it will work with everything else in your life too. The challenge as you get older is finding the friends you need around you. The right people won't always just show up; you'll have to go out and find them.

Crossroad:

Life has numerous intersections where you have to choose your direction and the people you'll travel with. Do you take the turn to follow people down their familiar road? Or do you grab ahold of people traveling a new and exciting road? Uncertainty will always create butterflies in your stomach. Don't be scared of those butterflies. Let them lead you.

3 Things You Need to Know Before Graduation:

- You never know how to do anything until you do! Don't waste your time uttering, "I don't know how." Instead, find somebody who does.
- Once you have an idea of what you want to do, seek out people who have already done it and ask them to teach you. Don't feel obligated to remain close to childhood friends. People will change, you will change, and that's a good thing.
- Many want to be the smartest person in the room; my challenge to you is to be the dumbest person in the room. You will begin to think and act like your friends do, so choose who you surround yourself with wisely.

Chapter 14

Others Ahead of Self

"The greatest good is what we do for one another."
~Mother Teresa

Surround yourself with people willing to trade one of their biggest moments for you.

Growing up in central New York, I always rooted for the Syracuse University football team. Some of my most special childhood moments came from attending games at their home field, which was named the Carrier Dome at the time.

As a child, I dreamed of being able to play on the football field inside "The Dome." As my athletic career progressed, it became pretty obvious by my freshman year of high school that if I was going to play on that field, it wouldn't be as a Syracuse University athlete. Instead, we had the unique opportunity to play on that field in high school because it was the venue for our local sectional championship games.

Let me introduce you to Travis Robbins. Travis and his twin brother Todd were exceptional athletes and have always been exceptional humans. They were in the grade below me, but we always played sports together growing up. Life presents us with biological siblings and also "brothers from another mother." The Robbins twins were the latter to me.

On the high school football team, I was the left-side cornerback, and my jersey was number 3. Travis was the left outside linebacker, and his jersey was number 10. Before every play, we communicated with one another after reading the offense's alignment. We defended passes together, gang tackled together, teased each other when somebody messed up, bled together, sweat together, pushed one another during wind sprints and weight trained during the offseason. For three years, we had one common goal, to win a sectional championship on the football field at The Dome!

Everything was set up for us to do just that heading into my senior year—Travis' junior year. We had a solid season the previous year and were returning all but a handful of starters. Our team was favored to win it all! The season started exactly as planned. We were 5-0 out of the gate and ready to knock off our division rivals to go 6-0. After that, two very beatable teams were on the schedule, and it would be off to The Dome to fulfill our childhood dream.

Everything was going great during that sixth game. We were up 23-7 at halftime. We got the ball to start the third quarter, marched down the field, made it to the one-yard line, and were poised to go up 30-7 and put the game away.

But here's a not-so-fun fact about life, sometimes when everything seems to be going great, suddenly everything crashes on top of you.

We turned the ball over in the end zone on that play from the one-yard line. They responded by scoring a touchdown on their next possession, another after that, another after that, and yet another after that. The final score was 40-23. We lost. I was crushed. In fact, I cried. I sat at my locker in full pads, head in my hands, just numb for thirty minutes. I couldn't move, didn't want to move, and didn't want to do anything. Everything we had worked so hard to achieve for several years was now over in an instant. *The dream of my maroon and white number 3 Grates jersey playing on that dome turf was dead.*

To this day, three decades later, I still get emotional thinking about that game and what could have been. And while countless life lessons occurred through this adversity, the point of this chapter is surrounding yourself with fantabulous friends. Friends like Travis Robbins.

Fast forward one year.

I was playing Division III football at St John Fisher College as a freshman. As seniors, Todd and Travis Robbins were now co-captains of the high school football team. They had the opportunity to finish what we had started, and they did! After an incredible regular season, the team made it to the sectional finals to be played at the Carrier Dome. Obviously, I would be there to root my brothers on. I knew it would be emotional watching them compete on that field without me, but I had no idea how emotional it would be.

The night before the game, Travis called me and said, "I have a special surprise for you tomorrow." Those words were part of a much longer conversation and didn't strike me at the time. His surprise did strike me when the team took the field, though. After working his entire childhood to play that one game at The Dome, Travis finally got to run onto the field for the first time, but he wasn't wearing his number 10 jersey. Instead, Travis got ahold of my number 3 jersey. He wore it and played his heart out that game as if I was there with him. He had taken one of the biggest moments of his life and shared it with me.

In life, you'll find plenty of *energy vampires*. These are people that will suck the life right out of you. They will take things from you, spread negativity, point fingers, and find fault in everything and everyone except themselves. You'll also find a rare breed of people who constantly put others ahead of themselves. One of my favorite mantras is: "Those who always give—will always have." My friend Travis gave me something special that day. That memory that will last a lifetime and didn't cost him a dime.

My challenge to you is to avoid the energy vampires, find friends like Travis and, most importantly, be the person always seeking opportunities to improve the lives of others. The secret to living is giving.

Crossroad:

At several moments in life, you will have the choice to do something special for yourself or by yourself. You'll also have the opportunity to give that something special or share that something special with somebody else. When you arrive at such a crossroads, do what Travis Robbins did, put others ahead of yourself.

3 Things You Need to Know Before Graduation:

- Life is filled with *peaks and valleys*. As soon as everything starts going well, disappointment will often follow. Don't stay in a valley for long; know that more good times lie ahead.
- Surround yourself with people who put your needs ahead of theirs, then reciprocate their good-will.
- Those who give will always have—and giving doesn't always involve money.

Chapter 15
Givers Versus Takers

"If you always give, you will always have."
~Chinese Proverb

Allow me to explain the *contrarian approach*. Simply put, when masses of people are all running one way, the contrarian runs in the other direction. When a large group is all thinking and acting the same, the contrarian explores opposite points of view and actions.

From a very young age, you were conditioned to take. You took food, the clothes you were given, and the home you lived in. You often wanted to take additional things you saw, like candy at the store, another ride on the merry-go-round, or a specific toy. More often than not, you got what you wanted—sometimes, it may have required a temper tantrum.

Like it or not, you were programmed to believe that taking was a good thing. This programming may have led you to a path of entitlement. Entitlement is when you feel like you deserve to be given things, even when you technically haven't earned them. This is a dangerous path that many adults never leave. My challenge in this chapter is to begin the process of rewiring your taker mentality. It won't be easy, but it will be necessary to create true happiness in your life. In a world filled with takers, the contrarian approach will ultimately lead you to a life of abundance. You see, the funny thing about the giving path is you don't actually lose anything. In fact, those who consistently give are the ones who ultimately get more of everything!

I know what you are thinking. . . If I have one cookie and my friend has no cookies, and I give my cookie to that friend, now she has one cookie, and I have none. So how do I have more?

It's normal for you to think this way because you have been programmed with conventional wisdom. Conventional wisdom lies to you and creates a scarcity mindset. This mindset will lead you to a place of fear, causing you to think, *If I give up my cookie, I'll never have another to eat.*

However, now that you're familiar with the contrarian approach, you'll have an abundance mindset. This mindset allows you to understand that the world is full of cookies. In fact, there are endless varieties, flavors, and sizes of cookies. You will always have the opportunity to eat more.

Remember Eddie Excuses and Successful Sally? Yes, the two with the lucky bamboo seeds. Let's revisit them in the school cafeteria.

Eddie and a friend are sitting at lunch. Eddie has one cookie and notices his friend has none. Eddie thinks *I can give this cookie to my friend, but then I won't have the cookie, and I really want to enjoy it.* So, Eddie keeps the cookie. While chewing, he finds the taste average. Eddie also notices his friend is bummed out.

Sally is in the same situation. However, she chooses to give her cookie to her friend. Her friend's genuine excitement and sincere gratitude bring Sally more joy than the cookie's taste ever would have. Then, an interesting thing happens. Two other people at the table witness what happened and realize that Sally no longer has a cookie, so they both offer Sally theirs.

Now, Sally went from one cookie to no cookies before having the opportunity to enjoy *two cookies*! Sally finds herself at a crossroads. She can accept one cookie, two cookies or neither of the cookies. Regardless of what she chooses, Sally has the one thing all humans desire in life—*control*. The decision is hers, and whichever choice she makes will now make her happy. It all started by being a giver, understanding the contrarian approach, and having a mindset of abundance.

There are three types of people on this planet, energy vampires, energy angels, and ham sandwiches.

Energy Vampires: A vampire sucks the blood and, ultimately, the life out of people. An energy vampire sucks the energy—specifically the happiness and good mood—out of a person. How do you know when you are around an energy vampire? Here are the warning signs—it's always all about them; they shame you and make you feel guilty for things; they are surrounded by endless drama; they always want to one-up you, and they diminish your problems while playing up their own.

Energy Angels: An angel is a good, kind soul who is always there for you offering unconditional love and support. Here are some ways to identify them—they listen to you; they invite others to join the group; they apologize when they are wrong, and they *forgive* when you are. They give up the spotlight so others can shine, and they want nothing in return.

Ham Sandwich: A ham sandwich consists of two pieces of bread, a simple low-flavored meat, perhaps mustard or mayonnaise and sometimes even cheese. A ham sandwich will satisfy your hunger, but it's not something that will get you excited or something you'll ever spend extra money to have. If you eat a ham sandwich, you'll think, *Meh, that was alright.* If you don't eat a ham sandwich, you'll think, *Meh, no big deal.*

What's the point, and how does this fit here?

The world is full of ham sandwich people. They stand at the crossroad and choose nothing. By choosing nothing, they choose not to be an energy vampire. Also, by choosing nothing, they choose not to be an energy angel. They aren't good, and they aren't bad; they are a ham sandwich. Predictable and boring.

Crossroad:

This is one of the most common crossroads you will encounter along your journey. It's also one of the most difficult choices you'll make. Following the crowd will always be the easiest option. It's safe. It's secure. It's simple. Just do what everyone else does and get what everyone else gets. Sometimes this turns out to be the right decision for you. However, the goal of this chapter is to help you realize there's always a different path to take. Yes, it's the path less traveled. When you choose this path, those in the large group on the easy path will make fun of you for it and question your decision. Remember, race results are determined at the finish line, not the starting line. Your chances of winning the race increase when you're in a smaller group.

3 Things You Need to Know Before Graduation:

- Avoid vampires—and don't be one.
- Seek angels—and look to be one.
- While it's okay to eat a ham sandwich once in a while, don't choose that as your lunch every day.

Chapter 16
Be Real, Avoid Comparison, Ditch Gossip

"A flower does not think of competing with the flower next to it.
It just blooms."
~Zen Shin

<u>Be Real</u>

I have 5,000 "friends" on social media. If I ran into all of them at the store this weekend, 4,327 wouldn't even take two seconds to say, "Hey, how are you?" Some *friends*, right?

Yet, when I post a picture on social media, I get mad when they don't like it. Do you know why they don't like it? Because most of them don't even like me!

Spoiler alert, brace yourself; this one is going to sting. . .

Eight out of ten of your *friends* on social media don't like you enough to say, "Hey, how are you," when they see you in the real world either. You know why? Because social media is not real. It's a robot-created universe driven by algorithms designed to tick you off and then suck you back in, only to tick you off again. It's a land of make-believe, filled with real humans using you like a lab rat to sell your strongest emotional triggers to the highest bidder.

Since this section's essential F-word is *Friends*, I won't dive too deep into the social media rabbit hole—although more will come soon. I'll just say this, don't chase *likes*. You will know who your true friends are once you take a break from social media. They are the people still calling, texting, and wanting to hang out with you. That's the kind of real-world approval you should seek.

Avoid Comparison

Comparison creates unhappiness within us. Eleanor Roosevelt once said, "Comparison is the thief of all joy." In nearly every area of your life where you find unhappiness, you will find comparison. So, to experience happiness, you must eliminate comparison.

Social media has taken this unhappy issue of comparison and put it on steroids. When we see somebody at a fancy restaurant, on an exotic trip, or out golfing with buddies—again, it's not their actions that make us unhappy, but rather how we feel when we compare their experiences to what we are doing at that moment.

If you are feeling stressed out, unsuccessful, or unhappy, this is likely the result of you comparing the success of others or the success you've personally experienced in the past to your current situation.

The solution is awareness. Be aware of what is causing you this unhappiness and force yourself to eliminate the comparisons. Embrace the moment you're in now. The perceived happiness and success of others should have no bearing on your present situation.

Yesterday is gone, and tomorrow may never arrive; the only true life we can live is in the present.

Root for others to live their best life.

Help others to live their best life.

Celebrate with others when they succeed.

However, under no circumstances should you *compare* what they have, where they are now and how they live to your life. We each have our storylines with our own heroes and villains. Whichever chapter the story of your life is currently on, embrace it. Your story is unique. Celebrate that, don't let it bring you down by comparing it to others.

Ditch Gossip

"Hey, what's the deal with Mark?" I asked this of a co-worker over the phone one day while at my first job out of college. Mark was our boss, and my co-worker answered my call on speaker phone, though I didn't know that.

"I don't know, what do you mean?" my co-worker replied.

"Well, he's been a real jerk recently. I do everything he asks of me, all of the time and then when I ask him for one favor, he tells me no," I explained.

The next voice I heard was *not* my co-worker's; it was Mark's. "Hey Scott, this is 'Mark the Jerk,' you know, the guy who always tells you no." I got a lump in my throat and felt a tingle in my stomach as my face turned red and my heart began to accelerate.

From that day on, my relationship was never the same with Mark. I violated a trust agreement by gossiping behind his back. Going forward, this left Mark wondering how many other people I talked to that way about him when he wasn't around.

This taught me a valuable lesson, one I'll stress with you here, so you don't make the same mistake. Nothing positive comes from gossip. Only the weak speak poorly about those who are not present to defend themselves. If you would be embarrassed and ashamed to have the person you are speaking about hear what you are saying—the way I was when Mark replied—then don't speak those words. Furthermore, don't pile on when others are gossiping. And, while saying nothing is better than something, it's still not the best option. The best option is to encourage others to stop.

Crossroad:

You just arrived at an intersection where you don't appreciate, like, or support another person's actions, words, or point of view. You have two different directions you can head from here. Let it fly! Let it be known to anyone who will listen—or even some that won't—how much you despise the person not in the room. Or, you can say nothing to anyone who isn't the person you have the problem with. If you feel compelled to speak your mind, then pick up the phone or visit the person and have a conversation.

3 Things You Need to Know Before Graduation:

- Your real friends are those who know everything about you and still love everything about you. There was no social media when I grew up, but there was still a strong desire for social acceptance and approval. This led me to do many things I normally wouldn't do in an effort to impress people who didn't truly like me. Identify your real friends and leave the rest in the *land of make-believe.*

- The only person you should ever compare yourself to is the person you were yesterday, and by yesterday I literally mean twenty-four hours ago. How you look, your job title, your bank account, your clothes, or the car you drive should never be compared to anyone else. The only thing to compare to is you—the you that lived yesterday. Ask yourself, "Are you a better version of yourself today versus yesterday?" If your answer is yes, everything else falls into place over time.

- Gossip is the enemy of progress. You can spend your time speaking poorly of others, or you can be a kind, compassionate, loving human, but you don't get to do both.

Section Summary:

Surround yourself with amazing, supportive friends. Give to others with no expectation of anything in return. Understand real life versus filtered fiction. Avoid comparisons as well as gossiping.

Can you do this?

Will you make this pledge?

Awesome!

Go to www.tribeofteens.com to hear Tyler and I chat about true friendships.

Section 5

FAMILY

Chapter 17

Unconditional Love

"The only way love can last a lifetime is if it's unconditional. The truth is this: love is not determined by the one being loved, but rather the one choosing to love."
~Stephen Kendrick

To give your love unconditionally is to do so without expecting anything in return. It's easy to utter "I love you" and mean it on a surface level, but not in its deepest form. To love another human unconditionally is to have the ability to say "I love you" and mean it with your whole heart. While it would be nice to hear those words spoken back to you, you don't need it.

I truly love our family unconditionally. It's not easy to give all of yourself to another human, expecting nothing in return. In fact, it's the scariest thing in the world to do. Don't play scared when it comes to love, and always keep your essential F-words in order. Your religious *faith*, or your *faith* in the higher power you serve, will always be number one on the list. When nothing makes sense or seems to be going right, your faith that will lead, guide, and comfort you.

The second most important essential F-word is *family*. Whenever things in your life are scary, confusing, unfair, or illogical, it's your family that you will turn to. These people love you unconditionally. They don't just say it; they mean it. When it's time to turn words into reality, these people would trade their lives to save yours. For some, these are blood relatives; for others, while they aren't related by blood, they share a family bond that is just as strong. Ultimately, any other person that you love unconditionally is your family.

How do you know when you love a person, or a person loves you at this level? Well, let's take a look at emperor penguins and how deeply they love.

A male emperor penguin will march day and night, continually over seventy miles—which isn't easy with those tiny legs—to find his soulmate. In fact, we think it's cute when we see a penguin sliding on its belly, but in reality, they are doing so because its little legs are exhausted and need a rest from the march.

Once the emperor penguin finds another to love unconditionally, the female penguin lays an egg and then leaves, returning to the water to feed. Now it's up to the male penguin to balance the egg on his feet, resting his body above to keep the egg warm. Should the emperor penguin wobble and uncover this egg for any extended period of time, it will freeze. Remember, these penguins are in Antarctica, on a giant open glacier. There's no shelter, the temperatures are below zero, and the winds can gust over one hundred miles per hour. How long does the emperor penguin warm this egg, protecting it from these extreme conditions? Two months!

As if the freezing, windy conditions weren't enough, the emperor penguin starves for over one hundred twenty days to care for this egg and then the newly hatched baby penguin until its mother returns. When the mother does return, she meets their new child, and the father leaves to feed on fish. Once full, he returns, and the family is officially united.

When it comes to family, commitment, and love, I challenge you to be like a penguin.

You will be a part of numerous groups throughout your life; I like to call them tribes. By now, I'm hopeful that you've already joined our *Tribe of Teens* online. You'll also have different tribes of friends, co-workers, sports teams, and many others. The names and faces will change within all of those tribes. People will enter and exit your life throughout the various seasons. However, the only eternal tribe you'll be a part of is your *family*.

Care for, protect, and love your family deeper than all others in your life. It's not always easy to do; in fact, nothing in life is. Because your love for family is so great and you give it unconditionally, oftentimes, your expectations are higher. These high expectations can lead to disappointment when family members fall short of your hopes. Hesitate to be critical and focus on being helpful during times like these. It's easy to take a family member's love for granted. We assume our bond is so tight that we don't always need to love and support one another. However, this isn't true. Understand the *Law of Familiarity*, which states that when you get exposed to a certain person, thing, or place for enough time, you become familiar with it. When you become familiar with that certain person, thing, or place, your appreciation for it dies down. In other words, you start taking it for granted. This happens to everyone, and it can affect any area of your life, but it's most common with family because you see them the most.

Always be there for family, the same way the emperor penguin balanced that egg, providing warmth. When we lose sight of the importance of maintaining a loving relationship with those who love us most, it's like waddling away from that egg and exposing it to harsh, freezing conditions.

Crossroad:

You'll find plenty of moments in your future when a family member will disappoint you. Please understand that the greater you love somebody, the greater this pain feels when they fall short of your expectations. You'll always have two options. . . You can *forgive*—plenty to come on forgiveness in our next chapter—or you can allow those negative feelings to fester. Please live your life as a loving, forgiving person, especially regarding *family.*

Another crossroads you'll encounter when it comes to family is offering your presence. Often you can make a quick call, send a text message, or drop by for a visit with a family member. Whenever possible, take the time or make the time for conversations. The length and whatever it is you share don't matter. The simple act of communicating lets your family members know you care, and that means the world to them.

And finally, when it comes to communication, say whatever is on your mind—good or bad. To be unclear is unkind. Your family deserves to know what you are thinking and how you feel. Don't hold thoughts in, especially when it comes to those you love the most.

<u>3 Things You Need to Know Before Graduation:</u>

- Unconditional love is the deepest, most meaningful love. Allow yourself to care for another human at this level. It's equal parts scary and exhilarating.

- Not all relationships are the same. You can like or even feel love for another, but those feelings can be prioritized. Don't treat all tribes the same.

- Almost everything in life is temporary, including our actual lives themselves. A family bond is the closest thing we have to permanent. Care for those relationships above all others.

Chapter 18
Traditions

"Tradition is not the worship of ashes,
but the preservation of fire."
~Gustav Mahler

When I was born, my grandparents owned a basset hound named Willy. Basset hounds are the cutest little ugly dogs. They have short legs, stay low to the ground, have long ears that they almost trip over while walking, and have very loving but droopy eyes.

While shopping for my first Christmas, my mother found a gift box with a basset hound that looked just like Willy pictured on it. One of the first presents I ever opened was inside the "Willy box." From that year on, it became a tradition that the last gift I would open was the one wrapped inside that box. Through the years, the box aged, just like we do. As it became older, it had rips and tears. By the time I reached my teen years, the box could no longer be wrapped using paper or tape. When I reached high school, that box itself became the gift my mother gave me.

The Willy box was a family tradition that strengthened the bond between my mother and me. I honestly couldn't name a single gift that was ever inside of that box, but each year it was that gift I was most excited to receive. Looking back, I now realize my excitement wasn't created by the gift or even the box, but rather *the tradition* and knowing I received another year to celebrate Christmas with my mother.

Family traditions are recreated year after year and become events you look forward to. These traditions provide comfort and security. Each year our lives change as we all go through different seasons.

Some of these changes are great; others aren't.

In some seasons, we soak in the sun; in others, we shiver in the cold.

But through it all, these family traditions give us hope and generate anticipation of something exciting. They provide stability in a world that never stops moving.

Because the holidays are on the calendar each year, it's easy to create family traditions around those dates, and that's great. However, family traditions can take place whenever you choose. As I reflect on your childhood, we did week-long camping trips with the Doolen family each summer, hiked up a mountain each fall, and went on our "boys baseball trip" to a different major league stadium every spring. Your "Grandma Mizzy" held a family Olympics during summer; at the Kiwanis charity golf outing, we'd all play together. We had our fantasy football draft gathering, the winter "Munson Bowl," and you've even started your own annual tradition with friends by camping on an island just north of us.

Some of our greatest memories, and pictures, are created through family traditions. These traditions force us to make time for specific events and enjoy the moments we have with one another. When a family member's time here on the physical planet ends, these traditions help us to remember them and keep their spirit alive.

Now that you are a teenager and gearing up for the next season of your life, I encourage you to remain part of these traditions and start some new ones as well. Take something that you are passionate about—something you truly enjoy doing—and find a way to involve others in the family to join you each year.

And finally, while it's important to honor our past, you never want to get stuck in it. Oftentimes we fall into the comparison trap when it comes to traditions. Meaning last year's event may have been outrageously fun, and that becomes your expectation for this year. However, this year's may be less fun—this happens partly because your expectations for it were so high when comparing it to the prior year. People change, the weather changes, and every new day is unique from the one that came before it; and that's okay. Treat each year within a tradition as what it is. . . a brand-new event surrounded by a new set of circumstances. Allow family gatherings from the past to forever live on their own as you remain fully present in whatever joy the current year's gathering offers you.

Crossroad:

Life gets busy, and you will consistently utter the words, "I never have enough time." You will find yourself pulled in numerous directions with your own career, family, and hobbies. At times you won't want to attend or help plan an upcoming family tradition. At this crossroads, I encourage you to reflect on all of the great memories you have from past family gatherings and ask yourself what life would be like without them. Always make time for the people who mean the most. Everything else can wait.

3 Things You Need to Know Before Graduation:

- Things that don't get planned; don't get done. Never assume something will just happen or come together. Actively plan the moments you most desire in life.
- As humans, we don't want to face our own mortality. We say things like "nobody lives forever," but then we believe we will. Never pass up an opportunity to be part of a family tradition.
- Take tons of pictures, *print* them, and save them. Just like people aren't with us forever, traditions will sometimes also end. The printed pictures you hold in your hand years later will help you relive certain moments and bring that joy back into your heart.

Chapter 19
Regrets

"Never regret. If it's good, it's wonderful.
If it's bad, it's experience."
~Victoria Holt

I 'm sure by now you've done a few things in your life that you regret. I'm also sure there have been a few things you regret not doing. Spoiler alert; for the rest of your life. . . plenty more of each will come.

People will tell you that they have *no regrets*. Personally, I think that's a lie. And to take it a step further, regrets aren't a bad thing to have. At their core, *regrets are simply recognition*. In every instance, you either recognize you did something right, something wrong, or you missed an opportunity to do something altogether. None of that is bad. It would be far worse to lack the self-awareness to recognize one of those three things had happened. When it comes to regrets, work on decreasing the things you do wrong and try to seize the opportunities that could go right.

The secret sauce to success with this process is calling a time-out. Don't be in a hurry to make decisions. Don't blurt out the first thing that enters your head. Call an *internal timeout* and ask yourself,

"Is this something I will regret doing or not doing?" The more decisions you make during those brief timeouts, the fewer regrets you'll have.

Since this is our section on family, I'd like to rapid-fire some common regrets, so you are aware of them:

- Don't go to bed angry at a loved one or family member. Letting disagreements, arguments, or hard feelings linger is a poor practice.
- Don't be afraid to apologize when you are wrong.
- Never miss an opportunity to tell somebody you love that you love them.
- Seek opportunities to bring joy into somebody's life.
- Take the time to make a call, send a text, mail a card, or drop by to visit when you can.
- Take that trip when the opportunity presents itself.
- Give family the benefit of the doubt, and cut them some slack when they aren't at their best.

You'll always have regrets. Even if you are self-aware and call those internal timeouts, you'll still think you could have done more, should have done more, or wish you could take something back. It's natural. The key is to create a bigger list of things you are happy you did do.

It's Not Always Good

Obviously, I've shared many of the positives regarding family. It's only fair that I quickly address the darker side of some family dynamics. An old—and kind of gross saying goes like this, "You can pick your friends, and you can pick your nose, but you can't pick your family." This is true. However, just because you are related to somebody by blood doesn't give that person the right to mistreat or abuse you in any form.

In situations such as these, it's common for people to justify this mistreatment with thoughts of, "Well, they are family. And you don't turn your back on your family." Every situation is different, and it would be impossible for me to give general advice to unique situations, so I won't. What I will say is this, everyone deserves the very best you have to offer, and you deserve the same in return. Don't keep yourself trapped in unhealthy situations just because your names are on the same family tree. It's certainly okay to try harder and offer more time to fix troubled relationships with family. Ultimately, don't be afraid to walk away. Remember, nothing in life is permanent. Walking away doesn't mean you have to do so forever. You can exit an unhealthy situation and still leave the door open.

Final Thought on Regrets

John Mayer wrote the song "Say" intended for a movie called, *The Bucket List*. In that song, Mayer repeats the lyrics "Say what you need to say" over and over and over again. He does this to drive home the point that the biggest regrets in life are rarely from the things we say but rather the words and thoughts we keep to ourselves.

Your thoughts and opinions are just as important as the thoughts and opinions of the person standing next to you. You're just as worthy of doing the things you want to do and visiting the places you want to go as the person across from you. Choose to do what you want to do, and say what you need to say while you can.

Crossroad:

When you have unconditional love for another human, the expectations increase. You want to be the best version of yourself for them, and you expect the same in return from them. With this comes increased failure because you've set an incredibly high standard with these family relationships. Because your love for family is deeper, the pain and frustration hurt more. When you arrive at crossroads with family, be aware of regret—recognize it. You have unlimited *internal timeouts*, so use them. Ask yourself, "Is this something I'll regret doing or not doing?" Answer your own question and then move forward accordingly.

3 Things You Need to Know Before Graduation:

- Regrets aren't bad, and you'll always have them. The key is to keep that list shorter than the things I don't regret list.
- That three-second pause to process situations before you act will determine the depth of your relationships with family.
- Not all members of your family will be good people. Not all members of your family will have your best interest in mind. If you are in an unhealthy relationship with a family member, know that you don't have to stay there.

Chapter 20
Legacy

"If you're going to live, leave a legacy.
Make a mark on the world that can't be erased."
~Maya Angelou

I f you and a friend are going to head out on an adventure to a place you've never visited this weekend—and I hope you do—what's the first thing that happens when you get into the car?

You enter the address of your destination into your map app, right? This way, you know exactly where you are heading step by step.

If you didn't enter your destination into your map app—or actually have a map—that journey would be much different. Essentially, you'd be playing a guessing game.

Our lives are no different than that situation. We already talked about setting goals and creating a vision for your future. Throughout this entire book, I challenge you to recognize crossroads so you can make decisions that will lead you to your best life. Whatever life you want to live, you can have, but first. . . you have to type your final destination into your map app.

In this chapter, I will challenge you to spend some time thinking about the one thing nobody wants to think about—death. Please think about a date at least eighty years into the future. Whatever date you choose, imagine reading your own obituary. One hundred years after the day you were born, what will be written about you to summarize your life?

Weird, right? It is, and I know from experience. In my freshman year of college, a professor assigned this task to me. And now I assign it to you. I encourage you to put some deep thought into this.

What names will be listed as people who loved you the most?

What level of education did you achieve?

What type of career did you have?

What were your hobbies?

What were you most passionate about?

Ultimately, what impact did you make during your time here?

After living a one-hundred-year life, how do you want it all summarized in five hundred words or less?

Writing your own obituary as a teen is a form of goal-setting and an efficient way to define your vision. Essentially you are typing your final destination into the map app of your life. So, let's bring this full circle and talk about three important concepts when it comes to family: legacy, "The One," and those who show up in the rain.

Legacy: People will tell you that *life is short*. I understand that even if we live to be one hundred and fifty, that's not a long time in the big scheme of things. However, when it comes to our individual lives, living is the longest thing we ever get to do, but all physical lives will end. The only parts of our lives that can last forever are our legacies. Simply put, our legacy is how we are remembered and what we are remembered for after our obituaries are written. Once you know what you want your legacy to be, then you can spend all of your living years making it come true. Think of a deceased person who made a difference in your life, still inspires you, or that you think about often. To you, that person is a legend. And legacies of legends never die.

The One: I'm a big fan and follower of Ed Mylette. Ed often talks about being The One in his family. He believes that *one* person in every family changes the family tree. Every wealthy family had a point in time when they were not wealthy. That wealth was created when The One showed up. Every famous family that you know, at some point, was not known until The One showed up. Every family has an identity that is often passed on from generation to generation, but then it all changes when The One shows up.

I'm here to tell you that I believe with every fiber of my soul that you can be The One if you choose. And, The One doesn't have to change the family tree around wealth or fame. The One is simply the person who is remembered for something that altered the direction of the family for generations to come; the person whose branch stands out on a family tree filled with dozens of names. Don't allow other family members' journeys, past or present, to determine your path. Don't allow your family's identity, good or bad, to dictate your life. Only you get to write the story of your life. You have every right and all of the ability to be The One person in the family who changes the tree. What an amazing opportunity!

Those Who Show Up in the Rain: One of my favorite books of all time is *The Slight Edge* by Jeff Olson—it's listed in the back of this book as one of my recommended readings. Jeff does a fantastic job of making the compound effect easy to understand. One of my biggest takeaways from his book was this section where he talks about funerals.

At the average funeral, I read, about ten people cry. I couldn't believe it. I had to read the paragraph over again to make sure I'd gotten it right. "Ten people—that's it? You mean I go through my entire life, spend years enduring all those trials and tribulations and achievements and joys and heartbreaks—and at the end of it there are only ten people in the world who care enough to show up and cry?" I went on to the next paragraph. It got worse. Once those ten (or fewer) people had yanked their hankies and honked their schnozzes and my funeral was over, the number one factor that would determine how many people would go on from the funeral to attend the actual burial would be. . . the weather. The weather? Yes. If it happened to be raining, 50% of the people who attended my funeral would decide maybe they wouldn't go on to attend my burial after all and just head home.

Just like Jeff couldn't believe this when he read it, I couldn't either. However, it did put things into perspective for me. Suddenly I flashed back to teenage me sitting in the college library during freshman year, working on my own obituary. It hit me like a ton of bricks:

- Who helped me most from the moment of my birth? My **family.**
- Who helped create all of those wonderful memories I have around traditions? My **family.**
- Who were the first people I mentioned while writing my own obituary? My **family**
- Who would be the ten people who cried at my funeral and would stand by my gravesite in the rain when all is said and done? My **family.**

I then asked myself, "Why am I spending so much time trying to please and impress everyone else?"

Crossroad:

The cool thing about the GPS function within your map app is that when it tells you to turn right, but you turn left instead, it simply recalculates and puts you back on the right path to get you to wherever you want to go. Life works like that as well. Just because you took a wrong turn doesn't mean you can't get back on the right track. You have your goals and your vision board. You now know how you want your obituary to read and what you want your legacy to be. You're going to be intentional with your decisions to make it all happen. But there will be wrong turns along the way, don't stress when that happens. Instead, trust the map you created and simply recalculate your route.

3 Things You Need to Know Before Graduation:

- You get limited years to live but forever to be remembered.
- The story of your family's past doesn't have to be the story of your future. You have the ability and every right to be The One who changes the family tree.
- You get to write the story of your life. The main characters will always be **family.**

<u>Section Summary:</u>

Love your family unconditionally. Create moments that make memories. Don't regret; just recognize and be the person you wish everyone else was. Regardless of your family's past, only you control the future. Legacies live forever. Live your life in such a way that your legacy becomes legendary.

Tyler and I share some behind the scenes stories about our family at: www.tribeofteens.com

Section 6

FORGIVENESS

Chapter 21
Forgiving Others

"The weak can never forgive.
Forgiveness is the attribute of the strong."
- Gandhi

Humans are flawed. You, me, business executives, teachers, religious leaders, construction workers, accountants, and local volunteers; everyone you meet is flawed. To meet a living, breathing human is to meet an imperfect work in progress.

You know those wild, sometimes seemingly crazy thoughts in your head? Others have them too.

You know that self-doubt nagging negative voice that tells you that you don't belong or you're not good enough? Others have that too.

You know that time you wish you hadn't said that thing or done that thing? Others have the same regrets.

You know that time you had an opportunity to do something that you really wanted to do, but fear held you back, and you didn't? Others have had those same missed opportunities.

We tend to think we are the only ones with specific struggles. Beware of the lying nature of your brain. It will lead you to believe that other people have things all figured out, that things just come easy to them or that they have more opportunities than you do. Well, they don't. They are flawed humans, imperfect works in progress, just like you.

Sometimes you'll be on the receiving end of someone else's imperfections. They will say things to you that later on they wish they hadn't. They will do things they wish they didn't. Immediately you will be upset or angry at them, and frequently your feelings will be justified. But here is what I want you to remember. . . *it's them, not you.*

Immediately you'll want to play the victim. You'll ask yourself, "Why me?" You'll tell yourself that you didn't deserve whatever they said or did. And you'll probably be right. You know why? Because, just like you, they aren't perfect. They are a flawed human, and they have things going on in their life that you cannot see and may not know about. . . *it's them, not you.*

Don't take other people's mistakes personally. Allow them the opportunity to apologize or take it back. And if they choose not to, then it's on you to forgive them for their mistake. Remember, holding a grudge only hurts you. Trapping somebody else's anger inside of you only punishes the most important person in your world, *you.* Forgive those who do you wrong and set yourself free emotionally.

Now, I'll also strongly encourage you to reflect on this ancient proverb throughout your life: "Fool me once, shame on you. Fool me twice; shame on me."

Read that again and again and again. Allow the depth of those words to sink in. Yes, everyone is a flawed human, and everyone makes mistakes. However, there is a big difference between a one-time mistake and a consistent pattern of bad choices. If you find yourself in a situation where you are a victim of any sort of abuse, you can still find forgiveness in your heart, but you need to eliminate that person from your life. There is a big difference between "Oops, I messed up" and becoming the consistent target of somebody's anger and abuse. Yes, humans are flawed. Yes, all humans deserve forgiveness. Yes, there are some really bad humans out there that you just need to distance yourself from.

People can only cause you long-term pain if you allow them to. Always give people the opportunity to prove to you who they are. Once you know who they truly are—their actions will speak louder than their words—decide if they are worth being around. Adopt a "you can't hurt me" mentality. You know who you are; you're an amazing human. You love and respect others. You truly care about others. You are working to improve yourself and help leave the world around you just a little better than how it was given to you. You understand that you are flawed, and now you understand that everyone else is too. When others do or say undesirable things to you, you understand that *it's them, not you.* Once you forgive them and move on—either with or without them in your life—they can no longer hurt you.

And the final piece of this forgiving puzzle is rooting for others. We live in a society that loves to compete. I love to compete, and so do you. Competition is healthy. It's our measuring stick for where we are now and shines a light on areas we need to improve so we are more prepared for future competitions.

But do you know how you can never lose?

Root for your competition.

Sounds silly, right?

But think about it. . . if you want others to succeed and be happy, then how can you ever lose?

I know what you're thinking; *why would I let the competition win?* Your mind might have gone immediately to sports. Perhaps you are picturing yourself in a 400-meter run during a track event. The gun goes off, and you jog instead of sprint because you want your competitors to win.

Nooooooooo, that's not what I'm saying here at all.

For clarity, I want you to win. You should want to win. While preparing for a competition, you need to do so with a championship mentality. You always give 100 percent focused energy towards everything you are about to do. And when that gun goes off and the race begins, you are now giving 100 percent max effort with every intention of crossing that finish line first!

However, after all of the focused preparation and giving all of your energy and effort to the event, if you do not win, it's okay to be upset, but be upset with only yourself and only allow those feelings to fester for a short time. The person who won that race didn't beat you, they were simply better than you at that moment, but nobody can beat you. You want everyone to give max effort; you are rooting for the best person to win. Oftentimes you won't be the best person at a given moment, but that's okay because you are the type of person who roots for others and applauds their maximum efforts.

Again, that was a sports analogy, but the same principles apply in business and all relationships. Help others become a better version of themselves, and you can never lose. Help others obtain the things they desire, and you'll always feel fulfilled. Root for others to win, and you'll never be defeated. Don't live for the results; you cannot control them. Instead, fall in love with the process. Do everything to the best of your ability, and whatever will be, will be.

Crossroad:

Bad things will happen to good people. Yes, you are a good person, and bad things will happen to you. Often, the bad thing that happens isn't your fault, and it won't seem fair. However, it did happen, and now you have two choices regarding your direction. You can be upset, react with anger, trap hateful emotions inside of you or hold a grudge. Or, you can forgive the person who wronged you and move on.

I completely understand that you won't want to do this at times. I get that much of what I've shared in this section is unnatural and difficult. However, that's why I wrote this book and why I strongly encourage you to be aware of and work to improve in these areas. Simply put, you can be the one who is "right" all of the time and play the victim who was "wronged," or you can be the bigger person who moves on to bigger things, but you can't do both.

3 Things You Need to Know Before Graduation:

- We think others have things figured out, but they don't.
- We believe when people wrong us, it's our fault, but it isn't.
- You can't be beaten when you have a *can't hurt me* attitude, a willingness to forgive and forget, and the ability to cheer on others in their journey.

Chapter 22
Your Personal Battery

"Dare to live by letting go."
~Tom Althouse

Take a look at the battery life on your cell phone. Is it fully charged? How often do you allow it to drain to the point where it completely shuts down and you can no longer use it? Not often, is my guess.

Let's say we are in a new city, and we are going to explore during the morning and then get bused an hour up the road to hike some scenic trails all afternoon. At no point along our journey will you be able to charge your cell phone. However, you'll want to use your cell phone on our way back home that evening. When we leave in the morning, your phone is 100 percent charged. All day long, you have to limit the phone's use to conserve energy and preserve the battery life.

Your emotional energy tank, or personal battery, is no different. Each time you get upset or allow something to bother you, a little energy is drained from your battery. It is no different than leaving an app open or downloading a large video. Those actions will continuously drain that cell phone battery—even though it's in your pocket. Holding grudges and not forgiving others or yourself does the same.

Choosing not to forgive will make you:

- Angry
- Unsettled
- Raw inside
- Want revenge
- Replay the incident or argument over and over

All of these are energy drainers and time wasters. They keep you from being the best version of yourself. Instead, be grateful. *You can't be hateful when you're grateful.* View every moment in your life, both good and bad, as what it truly is—a blessing. The more positives you find in each situation, the less negative effect it has on your energy tank. The quicker you can make peace with a situation and move on, the longer your battery remains charged. You already have all of the gifts required to succeed at anything you choose within you. Your mission is to activate those gifts and demonstrate your skills. A toy without batteries serves little purpose; make sure you keep your personal battery fully charged!

Crossroad:

Recognize when angry emotions set in. Indicators include increased heart rate, shaking hands, shortness of breath, and tingling in your stomach. Use these as warning signs flashing in front of you. If you pursue that anger, your battery will drain, forcing you to find a charging station. If you pause and think about the situation, you're choosing to conserve your personal battery life. That one deep breath during a three-second pause will change the direction of your life.

3 Things You Need to Know Before Graduation:

- Every choice we make either charges or drains our personal battery life.
- We cannot see the lessons in difficult moments as they are happening. Taking a break to reflect will provide your greatest education.
- Deep breathing is the strongest charging station in our world.

Chapter 23
Self-Forgiveness

"If you could kick the person in the pants responsible for most of your trouble, you wouldn't sit for a month."
~Theodore Roosevelt

When we forgive others, we forgive ourselves. When we hate others, we hate ourselves. How you think and feel about others directly reflects how you think and feel about yourself.

It's easy to identify others who messed something up, did us wrong or were unkind. We tend to judge them quickly and expect them to apologize by asking for forgiveness.

It's equally easy to know when we mess things up, do others wrong, or are unkind. Once we recognize our faults, we become remorseful and ask for forgiveness.

Now for the difficult part of forgiveness—*you* have to be able to forgive yourself. Just as holding a grudge against others festers negative emotions inside of you, so too will refusing to forgive yourself for personal wrongdoings. Remember, you are human; you are flawed. People will forgive you for mistakes, but it means nothing without your willingness to forgive yourself and move on.

Let me tell you a story. It was just before sunset on a hot evening in August. My best friend Chris and I, both thirteen years old at the time, were riding our bikes around town. We passed the basketball courts in the park when a well-known school bully, a senior on the football team I'll call "Meathead," yelled for us to come over to the courts for a second. Chris was the biggest kid in our freshman class, but not as big as this seventeen-year-old Meathead who wanted to show off in front of his crew.

"Hey, you think you're tough because you're the biggest kid on the freshman football team?" Meathead asked.

Chris sheepishly answered, "No," with his head down.

"Do you think you're tougher than me?"

This time my friend answered, "No, and we are out of here." He hopped on his bike and began to pedal away.

Unfortunately, he didn't pedal fast enough. Meathead sprinted after him, grabbed Chris by the back of his t-shirt and pulled him off of the bike. "Don't insult me by leaving before I was done talking to you," he yelled while picking up Chris' bike and slamming it to the ground. Now the bike was lying next to my friend when Meathead jumped up and down on it, destroying the tires.

Chris got up to stop him but was quickly pushed back to the ground.

Suddenly Meathead looked at me and asked, "How about you, little guy? Do you have something to say?"

My head went numb, and a tingling sensation ran through my fingers and toes. I was so scared I couldn't even speak. So instead, I ran! Well, I didn't run, but I pedaled my bike as fast as possible, fully expecting Meathead to be chasing behind, but he wasn't. However, my friend Chris was left alone, laughed at, and forced to carry his broken bike back home.

I was so mad at myself for running. I felt like I was the worst friend in the world. I couldn't sleep all night, knowing my best friend would never talk to me again.

But that's not what best friends do. Instead, they forgive and forget.

That next morning, I went to his house and said, "I'm so sorry."

He chuckled and asked, "What are you sorry about?"

"I left you. I didn't stick up for you. I just let it happen and then ran away scared."

He chuckled louder, "He would have killed you if you said something. That dude is a starting lineman on our varsity football team. He would have broken your ribs by poking you with two fingers. I don't care that you left. I'm actually glad he didn't get the satisfaction of punking us both down."

My friend forgave me, but I couldn't forgive myself. I replayed that event repeatedly and kept getting angry about all the things I could have done or should have done but didn't. I started hanging out with my best friend less because I was convinced that, deep down, he was really mad at me. I didn't show up to our optional freshman football summer training sessions because I was certain Meathead would seek me out and finish what he started that day.

In fact, it was close to half a decade later, our senior year of high school, when I brought that story up to Chris as we reminisced about good times and bad prior to our graduation. He looked at me and said, "You need to let that go, my man! I didn't care then, and I don't care now."

At that moment, I realized that my inability to forgive myself for a moment that didn't go the way I wanted caused me five years of unnecessary stress and anxiety.

Unfortunately, this isn't uncommon with humans. We do this to ourselves quite often. We spend all sorts of time and energy worrying about things we cannot change. Next time you are in the car, take a look at the front windshield. It's extremely large and provides a tremendous view of the road ahead of you. Then, take a look at the rearview mirror that's affixed to the windshield. That mirror is about 95 percent smaller than the front windshield. It's there so you can see what's behind you, the roads which you've already traveled down. Use that size ratio as a guide in your life. Focus on the 95 percent that's in front of you and if you have to look back, make sure it's only about 5 percent of your time. Otherwise, you'll miss the precious moments happening now because you were too busy trying to fix things from the past.

Crossroad:

Countless moments throughout your life will pass, and you'll look back in regret wishing you had or hadn't done or said certain things. There will be moments when you'll have to ask for forgiveness. Once you receive that forgiveness and you've spent some time in self-reflection and learning from this misstep, it's time to *forgive yourself*. It's time to move on in a positive direction. At this crossroad, you can choose the path of carrying baggage from your past or the path of self-acceptance. You are human; you are flawed, and you will make mistakes. Don't allow your history to hold you back from the shining star you'll be in the future.

3 Things You Need to Know Before Graduation:

- Beating yourself up over mistakes won't change the mistakes.
- Forgive yourself. Permit yourself to move on.
- It's okay to dwell on things for five minutes, but not five days or months and definitely not five years!

Chapter 24
Grudges

"Grudges are a waste of perfect happiness. Laugh when you can, apologize when you should and let go of what you can't change."
~Drake

D on't hold a grudge; it will only hurt you, not the other person.

Somebody did you wrong, lied to you, disrespected you, stole from you, cheated on you, just ticked you off or generated any other upsetting emotion within you.

It's done. It's over. Now what?

You're at a crossroad.

You can forgive and forget and move on in a healthy fashion. Or, you can hold a grudge. The grudge is the easier decision. *Don't build a life around easy solutions to complex problems.* Instead, deal with it the way it should be dealt with.

Even if you cannot verbally speak the words "I forgive you" to someone who did you wrong, type them. Perhaps that's a text or any other form of typed communication. If you prefer to write the words out on paper, do it. Even if you cannot deliver that paper to the person, still write the words; it's a start. Even if it's just forgiving the person in your own mind and wishing them happiness going forward, think it and mean it.

Grudges are a storage locker for your anger and ill will toward others. Nothing inside that locker will bring you happiness or move you forward in life, so throw it all away. The longer you let that locker sit in your brain and within your soul, the less space you'll have for more important things. Also, the longer it's there, the greater chance of it opening up in the future.

You are too amazing to carry pain from the past. *Forgiveness* will set you free and allow you to enjoy the view from life's high road.

3 Things You Need to Know Before Graduation:

- Don't carry other people's wrongdoings inside of you.
- Trying to figure out why certain people act a certain way is an exercise in futility, don't bother. Simply understand *it's them, not you* and confidently move on.
- Nothing will free your mind and soul faster than forgiving others, even when they may not deserve it.

Section Recap:

All humans are flawed. It takes strength to forgive people, forgive yourself, forget the past and root for others to succeed. A forgiving heart and an abundance mindset are a dynamic duo when defining your destiny.

Hop onto our Tribe of Teens website, www.tribeofteens.com, and hear Tyler share a personal story of forgiveness that helped him move forward in a positive direction.

CONGRATULATIONS!!!!

You are now two-thirds of the way through the nine *Essential F-Words for Teens!*

66.67% progress is an outrageously BIG deal!

Stand up, stretch out, and pat yourself on the back.
You now know the truth about **FAILURE**—it's NOT a bad thing.
You understand the importance of **FAITH**—believing good things will happen even when you don't know how, when, or why.
You are building **FOUNDATIONAL HABITS**—taking control of what you can control and consistently getting the little things right.
You can identify true **FRIENDS**—you become the sum of those you spend time with.
You have unconditional love for **FAMILY**—those who always have your back no matter what.
You see the value of **FORGIVENESS**—forget the past, and move towards a fantastic future.
Another deep breath. . .
Now let's dive into the next three sections:

FINANCES, FITNESS, FUTURE YOU!

Section 7
FINANCES

Chapter 25
House Money

"Never forget what happened to the man who suddenly got every-thing he wanted in life. He lived happily ever after."
~Quote from the movie Willy Wonka

For your eighteenth birthday, I feel like we should do something that an eighteen-year-old can do. Let's see. . . you can now go to war—okay, let's not do that. You can smoke—please don't do that. You can vote—that I would recommend, but not in October. You can gamble—okay, twist my arm. . . let's go to a casino!

My gift to you is $100 in casino chips for your eighteenth birthday. You and I sit down at a blackjack table, and the dealer begins to distribute cards. Just like all things in life, you win some hands, you lose some hands, and once in a while, you tie. With each new hand, you get a shot of dopamine—this is the chemical your brain releases to make you feel excited. After about twenty hands, you look down and realize you have twice as many chips as when you started. You now have $200 in front of you! It's at this moment that I give you your real birthday gift, a lesson on *house money.*

Take $100 of chips, put them in your pocket and keep them there until we leave. No matter what happens from this point forward, you cannot lose. A casino is commonly known as "The House." When you are playing with their money and not your own, you are playing with house money. This is when things get fun because you can no longer lose. Even if the dealer wins the next three hands—yes, they are taking some of the chips back, but it's their money, not yours. Your initial $100 is in your pocket, so the worst-case scenario is you break even. We got to spend time together, share a few laughs and walk out with the same amount of money we walked in with. When it comes to everything in your life—not just finances—I encourage you to play with house money as often as possible; *put yourself in as many situations where you cannot lose as often as you can.*

Easier said than done, I know. However, we've already established that an easy life is a boring, unfulfilling life. You are up to the challenge; I know it!

So, how do you accomplish this house money plan when it comes to finances? In the next three chapters, we will discuss the following topics.

- Avoiding the debt snowball
- Focusing on assets over income
- Taking calculated risks
- Having the courage to cut losses and start over
- Working with a plan

Before diving into that, I want to share how this house money mindset can serve you in other areas of your life beyond money.

I have a good friend and business peer named Brent Hershey. Of all of the conversations I've had with people in the business world throughout my career, this one particular conversation I had with Brent stands out above the rest. Shortly after I released my first book entitled *Insurance Agency Optimization*, Brent called me and said, "Scott, I read your book and loved it. It's my goal to write a book as well. However, my book will be much shorter than yours. In fact, my book will have more words on the cover than it will inside of it."

Intrigued, I chuckled and said, "Oh yeah, Brent, tell me more about that."

He replied, "I don't know exactly what the title will be, but it will be something along the lines of 'How to hit all of your goals and get everything you want out of life.' Once the reader opens the book, there will only be two words 'Just Ask.'"

It was at that moment I realized, as humans, we love to overcomplicate fairly simple things. I had written an entire book about how to succeed as an insurance agent, and my friend Brent summarized the answer in two words—just ask.

I share Brent's advice with you and incorporate it with the concept of house money because you cannot lose when you just ask for things in life.

Think about it. Before you ask a question, you do not have whatever it is you are asking for. So, if you just ask and the person says "No," what did you lose? Nothing.

$0 - 0 = 0$

You didn't have the thing you wanted (0), then you asked for it, then they said "No" (0), so the net result was zero.

$0 - 0 = 0$

But what if they said, "Yes!"

Then you would have whatever you wanted but wouldn't have gotten it if you didn't just ask.

That is house money. Nothing to lose, everything to gain.

Perhaps the most popular quote related to sports and business came from hockey player Wayne Gretsky who famously said, "You miss every shot you don't take."

Go back to the list I shared with you from the top regrets of the dying. How many of them said, "I wish I asked for fewer things that I wanted in life."

None.

How many regrets on that list involved not asking for more or trying new things?

Many.

Go back to section one on failure. Is asking or trying something new a fail if it doesn't work out as you had hoped the first time? No.

What if you arrive at a crossroads where you think to yourself, *I really want to ask this, but I'm afraid I'll be told no*, and then you don't ask. Is that a failure? Yes.

You are currently living life as a teenager. Statistically speaking, you have 80 percent of your life ahead of you. Play the remainder of those years with house money. Understand the only thing you have to lose is the opportunity to receive everything you want in life because you didn't ask. I encourage you to allow the two words from Brent Hershey's book to echo within your head for all of your years to come. . . just ask.

Crossroad:

No need to travel far for this one. We just discussed this crossroads. You will have countless moments where you're presented with the choice of asking for something you want or just taking whatever is given to you. In one direction, you will find the results of a proactive life. Down that path, you control your own destiny. In the other direction, you will find the results of a reactive life. Down that path, you will live the life others assign to you. Please believe with all of your heart and soul that you are worthy of everything you want. Understand that you cannot lose; you just have to ask.

3 Things You Need to Know Before Graduation:

- 0 - 0 = 0. Okay, so I'm certain you already know that, but now you must equate it to success and happiness as you march later in life. You cannot lose something that you never had.

- Don't be so hard on yourself. People like you more than you realize. We lie to ourselves by believing we aren't worthy of certain things, so we don't ask for them. Ultimately this only punishes you. You will receive far more than you realize if you just start asking for it.

- Life is way more fun when you pursue what you want versus making the best of what you're given.

Chapter 26
How I Lost $1,068,208 by Saving $100

*"Compounding interest is the greatest invention
the world ever produced."*
~Albert Einstein

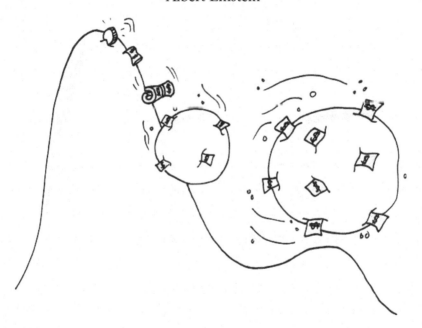

This entire book was intentionally written for you to create
awareness of opportunities and potential traps that lie ahead
in your future. The greatest gift I can give you as a teenager is
knowledge and insight into what your future days may look like based
on present-day decisions.

Every parent's wish is for their children's lives to be a better version of their own. I write this book for you and every other teen in your generation so you can learn from my mistakes. Be aware of the crossroads you will encounter each day and prepare to make whichever decision feels right for you at that moment.

In this chapter, I want to take you back to the summer of 1999, I wasn't much older than you are now. That spring, I graduated with a bachelor's degree and a month later started working my first full-time job—yes, I was adulting. And to prove just how much of an adult I now was, I listened to a co-worker who gave me some of the greatest advice anyone can give a young adult just starting their first job. . . begin investing your money.

My co-worker introduced me to her financial advisor. I scheduled an appointment and walked in, fully anticipating a roadmap to financial freedom! And, spoiler alert. . . I received it that day!

To provide a reference point, due to inflation, $1 in 1999 is comparable to $2 in 2023.

Also, I want to pause here to ask you a question that I'll discuss later in the chapter. Would you rather have $1,000,000 in your hand today or a penny today that will be doubled in value every day for the next thirty days? Think about that for a moment.

I was sitting at this financial advisor's desk during the summer of 1999, and I don't remember his name or the firm he worked for. I do remember he was a pretty chill guy, wearing a button-down shirt, sleeves rolled up, leaning back with his hands behind his head. He smiled as he spoke, rocking back and forth in his fancy desk chair. I'll never forget what he told me that day. He said, "Scott, at your age, if you consistently invest $100 each month from now until the day you are eligible for social security, you'll have one million dollars in your account. I've become the 'Johnny Appleseed' of a product called the

Roth IRA. If you put that $100 into a Roth IRA, you'll be eligible to take all of that money without paying any taxes by the time you retire!"

Now, I've always loved money, and I always wanted to be a millionaire—at the time, I had about $286 in my savings account, so he had my attention. My biggest question was, who is Johnny Appleseed?

To save you the Google time, John Chapman, better known as "Johnny Appleseed," was an American pioneer who introduced apple trees to large parts of Northeastern America in the early 1800s. He became a legend while he was still alive for his kindness, leadership, and generosity.

So, this investment advisor's gift to me wasn't going to be an apple tree but rather a plan I could use to take just a few dollars today and turn them into over a million tomorrow. I was sold. I opened my Roth IRA, funded it with my first $100 and left his office with a coupon booklet to mail in a deposit check for $100 each month until I turned 67 years old when I would finally have over one million dollars.

What happened next?

Well, I did mail in that check for $100 consistently on the first day of each month for an entire year. However, with each passing month, my excitement diminished. Towards the end of that first year, I kept thinking about all of the other things I *needed* that $100 for, and I became angry that I had to mail that check to the *Johnny Appleseed guy* with the rolled-up sleeves at the investment firm. Then, I became really upset when I received my first annual statement in the mail. I had contributed $1,200 into my account—$100 each month for twelve consecutive months. After one year, my account balance was $1,236.77.

Wait. . . WHAT??

After painstakingly sending that $100 every single month for an entire year, I had only earned $36.77 in interest?

I was angry. I felt betrayed. I thought Johnny lied to me. I wanted to quit. And I did. I stopped mailing that $100 check in each month, and I took my $1,236.77 back—this actually made my gain even lower because now I had to pay taxes and fees on the money.

For the next decade, I contributed nothing to my retirement fund. In my young, ignorant eyes, I was *saving* $100 a month. Well, I wasn't technically *saving* it because I was spending it. On what? You know, super important things I had to have—clothes, shoes, concert and ball game tickets, fast food, adult beverages, lotto tickets, video games, you know—all sorts of necessities!

By the time I reached my thirties, I no longer owned any of the things I had spent that extra $100 on; I also had nothing saved for retirement. But, no big deal, right? I still had thirty-plus years to catch up. Unfortunately, I found out I was wrong. Very wrong.

Without getting too deep in the weeds here, I want you to know that three primary factors that determine investment results, and we control only two of them.

Contribution: How much you invest each month.

Rate of Return: How much your investments earn or lose each month.

Timeline: How long you are contributing.

You can control ***how much*** you contribute.

You can control ***how long*** you contribute.

You *cannot* control the ***rate of return.***

I messed up when I was your age because I failed to comprehend the magnificent power of compounding interest. And I could never wrap my brain around the statistical fact that ***the most important piece of the investment equation is time.*** When I turned thirty-one, I didn't think skipping the ten years prior was a big deal because I still had thirty-six more years to invest before I turned sixty-seven, but here are the real numbers I soon discovered.

Age	Monthly Investment	Annual Return	Total at Age 67
21	$100	9.75%	$1,068,208
31	$100	9.75%	$396,863

I'm sorry, what? Talk about being mad! By *saving* that $100 each month in my twenties, I cost myself $671,345.

But wait, it gets worse. Now I was thirty-one years old. I was married, owned a home—with a large mortgage—had a car payment, credit card debt—more to come on that soon—student loan debt, and two babies under the age of four. Now I really didn't have an extra $100 to invest—at least, this is what I told myself. So, I waited.

What ultimately happened is that if I wanted to have over a million dollars by age sixty-seven, as a thirty-one-year-old, I would have to invest $271 per month because I had less time. Check out the chart below. By the time I got to forty-one years old, look at how much I'd have to contribute each month to land over one million.

Age	Monthly Investment	Annual Return	Total at Age 67
31	$271	9.75%	$1,069,861
41	$750	9.75%	$1,061,667

Yup, you read that right. At the age of forty-one, when I finally felt ready to contribute that $100 each month that Johnny Appleseed had encouraged me to invest twenty years earlier, I would need to invest $750 monthly to accumulate over one million. Why? Because we only control two factors in the investment equation—time and contribution. Because I allowed so much time to pass, now I had fewer years to age sixty-seven, so the *only factor* I could now control was my contribution.

This is the amazing power of compounding interest. The number one factor all investors have when building wealth is time. This has been the case since Albert Einstein deemed **compounding interest the greatest invention ever.**

One last visual in this super important chapter. Picture yourself at the base of an Olympic-sized mountain. It's outrageously high. You actually strain your neck, trying to look up to the top of it as you stand there in the snow. Now, you jump onto a ski lift and ride to the top of that mountain. You climb higher and higher and higher, and suddenly you notice you are above the trees. You continue to ascend and notice birds flying below your feet. You keep climbing higher and higher and higher, and now when you look down, people on the ground look like little ants. Finally, after twenty minutes, you reach the top of this mountain. With two hands, you form a snowball no bigger than the size of a baseball. From the top of this mountain, you get down on two knees and give this little snowball a soft push, sending it rolling down.

What happens to this snowball as it rolls down the mountain? It gets bigger and bigger and bigger and bigger. It picks up more snow with each rotation and picks up a little more speed as well. By the time it reaches the bottom of the mountain, it is this mammoth snow boulder with outrageous momentum that cannot be stopped. And to think, it was just a tiny snowball at the top.

Now, I want you to picture a snowy hill you used to sled down as a kid. No ski lift required; you can walk to the top of this hill. Sure, it feels steep for your legs, and they burn as you climb to the top, step by step. But within a few minutes, you reach the top of this hill. Again, you fall to your knees, and with two hands, create a snowball the size of a baseball and push it down the hill. Same thing happens. The little snowball picks up more snow with each rotation and picks up speed along the way, but very quickly, that snowball reaches the bottom of the hill and stops. Sure, it's a bit bigger than when it started at the top, but not much, and nobody really notices a significant difference.

I'm guessing you've connected the dots with this metaphor. If not, I'll elaborate because this one principle can make you a millionaire and beyond if you have the patience to do what I failed to do when I was your age. You are in your teens, staring up at that incredibly gigantic mountain right now. Each year, that mountain is going to get just a tad shorter. Twenty years from now, it will have turned into that hill you used to sled down as a child. Forty years from now, it will just be flat ground. The size of the slope is the time you have to invest.

The snowball is the amount of money you have invested. How big that snowball becomes at the bottom is primarily determined by the size of the slope when you decide to drop to your knees and give it a push. The longer you have to invest, the more money you will earn.

You will always perceive that you have better or more important things to spend your money on when you are young. My wish for you is that you take all the advice I share in this book to heart. However, it's this one concept I hope you dive even deeper into from now through forever. *The power of compounding interest is unmatchable.* Make sure you start paying Future You now. You won't regret it, I promise!

Hey, remember that choice I gave you earlier in this chapter about the $1,000,000 now or the penny doubled every day for thirty days? Which did you choose initially? And, has your answer changed now that you've been introduced to compounding interest?

Here's the penny's path as it made rotations down that mountain…

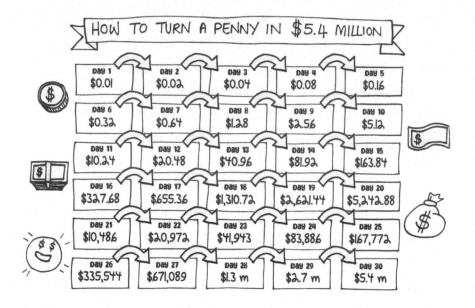

Crossroad:

Each day you will make decisions on how to spend your money. Remember that every spending choice today comes at the sacrifice of something else tomorrow. Your challenge at this crossroads is to force yourself to fund your investment account if you can. Do not skip that investment for something trivial.

Sacrifice the new shoes, fast food, or computer games. At this crossroad, you'll have the choice to spend your money on something you'll briefly own or follow the direction that provides a potential source of future income and legacy.

3 Things You Need to Know Before Graduation:

- Always pay yourself first. If you have $100 to invest monthly, make that the very first check you write. Nobody is more important than you—or Future You. Invest in yourself financially first, and pay everyone else second. Have fun with what's left third.

- The longer you wait to invest, the more painful it becomes in the future.
- Time is the greatest asset you own, and no amount of money can buy it back. Leverage all of the time you have to invest. Start now, and don't quit!

Chapter 27
Assets Over Income

"Wages make you a living; profits make you a fortune."
~Jim Rohn

What is an asset?

Think of anything you own that has value. If you can trade something right now and receive money for it in return, that is an asset. Examples of assets include:

- Cell phone
- Computer
- Gaming system
- Jewelry
- Collectibles
- Musical instrument
- Clothes and shoes
- Tools
- Sports equipment
- Car
- Cash, Bonds, Crypto, IRA
- House
- Land

Pause here and take a moment to list everything you own that you could sell if you needed money. List all of your personal assets.

Now that you understand what an asset is, it's crucial to understand the difference between an appreciating asset and a *depreciating* asset. Simply put, an appreciating asset has a strong chance of increasing in value over time. A depreciating asset will likely decrease in value over time.

With this new understanding, go back to the personal asset list you created and put a star next to the items you can currently sell for more money today than you purchased them for. Also, put a star next to the items you believe will have a higher value in the future than you initially paid.

Congratulations! You just identified all of your appreciating assets—everything you own that can make you a profit today or in the future.

In this chapter, I challenge you to become an Appreciating Asset Collector.

Our society gets so caught up in income—the money earned from working. In the quote that starts the chapter, we learn from Jim Rohn that *wages*—the amount of money you earn at work will make you a living. However, *profits* will make you a fortune. What does he mean by profits?

Profits are the difference between what you paid for something versus what you sold it for. For example, if you purchase a home for $200,000 and five years later sell it for $250,000, you earn a $50,000 profit. If you buy one hundred shares of a stock at $20 per share, you have stock valued at $2,000. If the stock price increases to $30 per share, you now have stock valued at $3,000. If you sell the stock, you earn a $1,000 profit.

On the opposite side, if you consistently purchase depreciating assets—look at everything on your list that does not have a star—you will realize a loss. For example, you purchase a new gaming system for $400; one year later, you sell it for $200. Your balance sheet just took a $200 loss in profits.

It's also super important to pause here and add the disclaimer that all investment products, including real estate, come with *risk*! Home prices can go up, they can also go down, and over time they will do both. Stock prices can go up, they can also go down, and over time—they will do both. So, please understand—as an Appreciating Asset Collector, the risk involved.

Also, understand you only take a loss on an asset when you sell it. So, if you buy that home for $200,000 and suddenly homes comparable to yours are selling for $175,000, you do not realize that loss unless you sell. If you continue to own that home for the next five years and then want to sell when comparable homes are selling for $225,000, you have the opportunity to realize the gain. So, you can buy or sell assets, but you can also practice the investment strategy of holding them, and that's what most Appreciating Asset Collectors do.

Remember, you are the chief executive officer (CEO) of "Me, Inc." Your life is your business. Be proud of the products and services you own and sell. Be proud of your bottom line and work hard to become profitable each month while focusing on growing your asset portfolio for the future.

In the business world, you'll hear the term P&L statement quite often. This refers to a company's profit and loss statement. Essentially on one sheet of paper, you can determine if a company is strong or weak financially based on its P&L statement.

I'd like you to pause here and create your own personal profit and loss statement.

You already listed all of your assets. Please review it and ensure your checking and savings account values are also listed. Add a value to your assets—how much could you sell that asset for right now?

Next, make a list of everything you spend your money on and how much you spent on each asset or currently owe. That list your debts.

Next, add up the value of all of your assets.

Add up the figure for all of your debts.

Subtract the debts from assets.

The resulting figure will provide you with your "net worth." This could be a positive or negative figure. I encourage you to update this on the first of each month. Focus on getting your net worth as high as possible. Focus on assets over income. The things that become our obsessions will become our possessions. Keep your P&L statement in front of you and balance it monthly. Your consistent focus on it will help you make better financial decisions each month.

Be aware of "emotional finance" when it comes to money and, specifically, when collecting assets. What would you say if I asked if you would rather buy something at a low price and then sell it at a high price or buy something at a high price and then sell it at a low price? Obviously, you would answer buy low and sell high. This philosophy creates profits, helps your P&L statement, and increases your net worth. That's a simple answer to an easy question. However, most humans on this planet do just the opposite!

Why?

Because we allow our emotions to get in the way. Remember when we discussed *recency bias* in Chapter 6? To refresh your memory— recency bias is our belief that whatever is happening right now will continue to happen forever. We think whatever we are experiencing today—good or bad—will never end. However, it does. It always does.

Everything is temporary. And it has since the beginning of time. Each morning the sun comes up, and each evening the sun goes down. The ocean waves crash in, then they get sucked back out. When spring ends, summer begins, then fall arrives, followed by winter, then it's spring again.

Ironically the financial markets are no different. There are peaks and then valleys. Things go up, and then they go down. Look at any asset that you want to purchase and go back one hundred years, and you'll see a consistent pattern of ups and downs. Those who win and realize the highest long-term profits are those who continue to *buy and hold* regardless of the ups and downs.

Here is an example of how your emotions can punish you in finance...

Let's say all of your friends are buying a new crypto coin called "Moon Coin."

It only costs a penny per coin. Your friends are buying tens of thousands of these at a time! Suddenly the value of the coin goes to two cents, then three, and then four. Your friends can't stop talking about how they have doubled, tripled, and some even quadrupled their initial investment in just a few weeks. Eventually, the value of each Moon Coin goes to ten cents, and a buddy of yours who invested $10,000 when it was a penny sees his portfolio rise to $100,000—wow! He is legit *over the moon excited.*

You think to yourself, *I want in on this too*! You take $10,000 out of your savings and invest it all in *Moon Coin* at ten cents per coin.

You are ready to become rich! Watch what happens next...

The coin value drops the next day to nine cents.

A week later, eight cents.

Two weeks later, seven cents.

A week after that, six cents.

Whoa! What is happening here? A month after investing $10,000 and expecting to have $100,000, you now only have $6,000.

You are angry.

You are scared.

You only had $10,000 total in your savings account; now your account is empty, and your crypto portfolio has lost $4,000 as well. You start thinking, *What if this keeps dropping? What if it goes all the way back to a penny where it started? What if it goes to zero?* Gulp! Gut check time. Do you know what the majority of people do in this situation? *They sell for a loss!*

You decide to sell too. You cut your losses, take the $6,000 and put it back into your savings account. You are outrageously mad about this, as you should be. You just *bought high* (at ten cents per coin) and *sold low* (at 6 cents per coin).

It's the exact opposite way you answered my initial question just moments ago.

Want to play this scenario out and make you feel even worse about your decision? Let's do it.

One year after selling at six cents, your buddy asks, "Are you still holding that Moon Coin you purchased last year?"

You tell him you sold at six cents and wonder why he's asking. His shoulders drop, and he puts his hand on his forehead as he breaks the news to you. "Ugh, it just hit twenty cents per coin!"

At that moment, you realized that you allowed your emotions to get the best of you. You took one bad month and forced yourself to believe it would last *forever,* and you sold low. Had you held that investment, you would have doubled your money a year later. And that is how *emotions can disrupt your financial plan.*

Warren Buffet is widely regarded as one of the smartest investment minds of his generation, and his portfolio backs that up to make him one of the wealthiest people in America. He famously said the key to investing is, "Be fearful when others are greedy and greedy when others are fearful."

A simple translation to this is to do the opposite of what most humans do because most humans fall into that emotional trap. When everyone is buying—pricing is high—be fearful. When everyone is selling—pricing is low—be greedy. Live by Warren Buffet's philosophy.

Another Disclaimer Here: Please consult with a financial professional before making any investments on your own. I am sharing high-level concepts in this book and using *oversimplified examples* to help you understand concepts. *This is not intended to be a personalized investment strategy.* Everyone is in a different place, with different goals and different timelines. Please consult a financial professional before investing and/or accumulating assets because the risks in this space are real!

Finally, let's talk about the greatest asset you have. It's You! The greatest investment you can make is an investment in yourself. I already know you are willing to do this because you are still reading this book. Eight out of ten of your fellow teens have stopped reading by this point, but not you. You see the value in investing in yourself, and you have the desire to be part of our Tribe of Teens who are dedicated to improving themselves and the world around them.

Keep reading quality books.

Keep listening to podcasts that will improve you.

Attend seminars that will open your mind to new possibilities.

Attend college classes that will educate you.

Hang around people who are more experienced than you.

Hang around people who dream big and will inspire you to do the same.

The bottom line to your *bottom line* when it comes to finances is—invest in yourself. You are the biggest asset you own. *The more you learn, the more you will earn.* Knowledge and experience cannot be taken away from you. Jobs may change, businesses may fail, and you will have many ups and downs, successes and setbacks, but ultimately, you'll be better for all of it. Keep learning, keep dreaming, keep implementing, keep track of your results, and you'll keep thanking me for this knowledge long after your teen years, I promise!

Crossroad:

Long-term, conservative investing is boring. I'm not going to sugarcoat that fact. This is especially true at your age. When you begin collecting assets in your late teens and early twenties, you'll want to immediately receive the rewards and big payoffs. However, that's not how this game works. This is a loooooooooooooong game. Remember, life is not short; it's the longest thing you'll ever do. Knowing this, you have to prepare to play this game for a loooooooooooooong time. And, from an investment standpoint, it's flat-out boring! However, now that you know this, you will be prepared for the numerous crossroads where you can chase new, exciting, get-rich-quick types of opportunities. Or, you can stick to the slow, steady, long-term, boring approach to asset collecting and holding. I'm here to tell you that while every fiber in your body will want to chase the latest and greatest new opportunity—the smartest and wealthiest people on the planet are traveling down the slow, steady, boring road. Join us, won't you?

3 Things You Need to Know Before Graduation:

- Work with an investment advisor or financial professional to help you structure a plan that Future You will be proud of and appreciate.

- Dare to be different. When the masses are all walking to the left, that's a good sign that you should be running to the right! If you want the results that only 10 percent of people get, you must do the things that 90 percent of the people are unwilling to do.

- Don't take financial advice from people who are broke. It's wild how many people in your life will act like experts and offer their advice and opinions on subjects they know nothing about. Seek out people who have been there and done that. Ask those people how they did it.

Chapter 28
Avoid the Debt Snowball

Yes, I did just start back-to-back chapters with similar quotes from Albert Einstein. I did this for two reasons: first, Einstein is widely regarded as one of the most brilliant minds to live over the past two centuries, and second, he was fascinated by this simple concept of compounding.

Remember, with every small, simple, *positive* action we take, we cast a vote for our future. With every small, simple, *negative* action we take, we also vote for our future. It's crucial we vote today for the way we want our future to look tomorrow.

My experience has taught me that the amount of debt you take on during the seven years following high school can dictate the levels of success and overall happiness you experience for the rest of your life. Those who bury themselves with debt before the age of twenty-five often spend their entire career working jobs they don't necessarily like, but feel locked into because they have large bills to pay. They cannot pursue their passions, take chances, explore other opportunities, or experience new adventures because they are crippled with debt. Large bills and excessive debt makes you a prisoner to your past, limits your future, and adds unhealthy amounts of stress to your life. I work with countless people in their forties and fifties who have been working their tails off in jobs they don't like, going paycheck to paycheck in an effort to just catch up. When they finally dig out and start to get ahead, now they have an "it's too late for me to make a change" mentality and end up retiring after having missed opportunities during the greatest years of their life. Why? One word—debt.

Conversely, those who can avoid debt play the game of life with house money—remember Chapter 25? True freedom is the ability to make your own choices, pursue your passions, and not owe anyone anything beyond your means. Living life without debt—or very minimal debt, allows you to choose the work you do, take chances, seek new opportunities, and be adventurous. Avoid debt and live life on your own terms.

For this exercise, instead of putting your investment money in a bank, I'm going to have you put it in a bucket. In this example, the money you earn will be converted into gold coins valued at $100 each. Now you are going to walk five miles carrying your bucket. At the end of each five-mile walk, I will place one gold coin in your bucket. You will take these five-mile walks as often as you'd like for the next year. Some days you may decide to walk ten miles and receive two gold coins. Other days, you may rest, choosing not to walk at all. The choice is yours. You also have another very important choice. You can collect your gold coins in a bucket with a seamless, solid bottom. Or, you can collect your gold coins in a bucket with holes in the bottom. And those holes are larger than your gold coins. Oh, and by the way, once one of your gold coins falls out of that bucket, you cannot have it back until you walk another five miles. Which bucket are you choosing? The solid base, I'm sure.

If you choose the bucket with holes, you would have to walk and walk and walk every single day, all day long, to collect gold coins that you lose. By the end of the year, you will have worked your butt off and earned tons of gold coins, yet when you look into your bucket, you have nothing. You are right back to where you started, and now you have to keep walking.

The walking is you working. Whatever you decide for a career, you will have to put the work in. You will be rewarded for the value you bring to the workforce and the people your products and services support. In return, you will be compensated.

The gold coins are your income. You worked hard and delivered tons of value; you were compensated for your efforts.

The holes in your bucket represent your debt, the bills you have to pay. Simply put, the less debt you carry, the fewer holes in your bucket and the more gold coins you can accumulate.

Sounds simple, right? Well. . . it's not. However, by the end of this chapter, you'll be aware of this dangerous debt crossroads and be prepared to make solid long-term decisions that will ultimately benefit Future You.

Burn these words into your brain forever, *"When it comes to earning money, the most important factor is not what you earn, but rather what you keep!*

I have met and coached numerous professionals who earn over $500,000 annually but do not have $500 in their checking accounts. Why? They spend more than they make. Who would you rather be? The person who earns $500,000 and gets to retirement with $50,000 in their account? Or, the person who earns $50,000 and gets to retirement with $500,000 in their account?

You live during an amazing time when it is incredibly easy to make money. You also live during an amazing time when it is incredibly easy to spend money. This new digital age is a dream for advertising and marketing companies. Whether you realize it or not, everything you do while holding a cell phone, iPad, or typing on a computer is being tracked—and I mean everything. Big technology companies are worth billions of dollars because they collect and sell your data to advertising and marketing companies. Advertising and marketing companies are worth billions of dollars because they are ninja-like at creating content that plays off of your deepest emotions.

This is called behavioral marketing. If you and I both enter a word into a search engine, we will receive different results based on what that search engine knows about us and what we like—or dislike—seeing. Our social media news feeds are different. The advertisements we see are different. *None of what you see is a coincidence; you're intentionally targeted.* All in an effort to extract gold coins from your bucket.

I believe it's crucial with all things in life to focus on controlling only the things you can control. You aren't going to stop behavioral marketing, and you aren't going to stop using cell phones or computers. So, what can you control? Your awareness. Just understand how this works and why it's happening. Take a moment to pause, reflect and then make the best possible decision. The key is to avoid impulse buying. Impulse buying happens when you see something and you love it—and they know you will—so you immediately tap the screen or click the mouse to purchase it. Boom—instantly, your credit card is charged, and a gold coin falls from your bucket.

But was it just one gold coin?

Let's now go back to the opening quote. "Those who understand interest earn it;" we covered that in the last chapter with the snow boulder steamrolling down the gigantic mountain. "Those who don't understand interest pay it," this is another snowball we can create throughout our lives, but at the bottom of this hill, it's not good to have a snow boulder because this one is debt—money you owe to others.

Let's stick with our $100 scenario and say you charge something onto a credit card. At the end of that card's billing cycle—usually about a month—they will send you a bill for $100. If you pay that bill in full—you pay no interest. You spent $100, and then a few weeks later, you paid $100. In this example, you have no debt and pay no interest. *This is the financially responsible way to manage your credit card.*

However, there are options for paying credit cards. When they send you that bill for $100, they send it with two payment options. You can pay it in full like we just discussed, or you can make a minimum payment. If your full bill is $100, your minimum payment will probably be $15. You look at this bill and think, *Cool, $15 sounds better than $100; I'll just send that.* Now you have to pay interest—let's call it 14.9 percent—on the remaining $85.

The next month you haven't charged anything new on your card and receive a bill for $87.51 with the same option to pay $15. That's the choice you make. Now you are paying interest on $72.51. In this scenario, it will take you eight months to pay off that $100 purchase. Once interest is factored in, that purchase costs you just over $120. That $20 in interest that you paid is now $20 you didn't have to invest, so you also lost the opportunity to *earn interest* with that money.

You're probably thinking, *So what? It's only $20!* And you'd be right—if that was the only thing you ever charged to a credit card for the entire year. But what if you charged $100 every month and only made the minimum payment?

Now you have charged $1,200 in a year, and at the end of that year, making the minimum payment, you will have paid $180. But you'll still owe $1,225. Yes, you read that right. You will owe more than you charged, and you are out the $180 in minimum payments you made.

Those who understand interest earn it. Those who do not, pay it.

Let's finish this thought. What if—rather than charging $100 each month for a year to impulsively buy stuff you really didn't need, you invested that money instead? Remember, after one year of paying the minimum on a credit card, you spent $180, and now you owe $1,225. If you pay that balance, your $1,200 in purchases costs you $1,425 for the year.

Now let's look at the investment side of that $1,200 after a year. Let's say you earned 6 percent interest. Now you would have $1,272 in your account. Not only did you save the $225 in interest by not charging your credit card, but you earned $72 in interest. After one year, you are already $297 to the positive! But let's carry that $1200 investment out for the next thirty years, shall we? Compounding interest will turn that $1200 from this year into $6,892 thirty years from now!

The question becomes did you spend $100 a month to buy something for twelve consecutive months? Or did you cost yourself the opportunity to have an additional $6,892 in the future?

Every financial decision you make today comes at the expense of something else in the future.

Here are a couple of quick points on credit cards. I used an example of 14.99 percent as an interest rate. However, when you are young and starting to establish credit, oftentimes, interest rates can be as high as 25-30 percent! Also, many credit cards carry an annual fee you must pay just to allow them to charge you their interest rates. And finally, in these examples, I used $100 in monthly purchases. What if you are charging $1,000 each month? Now take the numbers I shared and multiply them by ten! This is how you create a *debt snowball*—the *biggest financial mistake you can make.* On top of that, you are being targeted to make these mistakes by billion-dollar companies every single day.

Credit cards are known as *revolving debt.* This means there is no contractual end to the payback period. It ends when you finally pay off the total balance rather than the minimum monthly payment.

The other type of debt to be aware of is *installment debt.* The most common installment debts are home mortgages and automobile loans. Now, a home is considered an *appreciating asset.* Meaning over time, the value of the property you purchase typically increases. An automobile is considered a *depreciating asset.* Meaning, over the course of time, the value of the vehicle decreases. Knowing this, be aware of how automobile loans can significantly contribute to your debt snowball.

Everything I'm sharing with you in this book is designed to help you create awareness. This way, when you reach any crossroad we discussed, you say, "Ah-Ha! I know what's happening here."

I've been in the sales industry for over twenty-five years. Here is one thing every salesperson knows and something you need to know as well...

Humans make buying decisions based on emotion, not logic.

Your five senses—taste, sight, sound, smell and feel—will release numerous emotions within you that will cause you to make irrational decisions at times, and the sales industry capitalizes on it.

One of the most emotional and irrational decisions we make is car buying. The first thing every car salesperson wants you to do when you visit is test drive a car. Why? Because a test drive releases all sorts of emotions within you and floods your brain with excitement!

You love the way the car accelerates.

You love the way it handles turns.

You love the way it looks.

You love the way you look inside of it.

You love that new car smell.

You love this car!

And as a result, you no longer want to drive your current, old car. Now that the salesperson has you on an emotional, sensory overload, she convinces you that the $500 payment for the next six years is no big deal. And you buy the car! Here is what you need to know about a new car. In two years, it'll be a used car. It will be old to you, and if you took out a loan for six years, you still have four years left on this used car and all of those emotions you had when you purchased it are gone. But do you know what isn't gone? That $500 monthly payment.

I get it. You have to have a car. And yes, you need a reliable car. My challenge to you is this—if you are going to take out a car loan, borrow less than you can afford. Let's revisit our two mountains, shall we?

The *pay interest mountain* has you spending $36,000—$500 per month for six years. That's $36,000—on a vehicle that may be worth

$10,000 at the end of that loan. What if you found a reliable vehicle for only $300 per month and could pay it off in three years? The total payout for that would be $10,800—$300 per month for three years; that's $10,800. At the end of this loan, perhaps your vehicle is worth $5,000.

Option A: $36,000 in payments, and the vehicle is worth $10,000, net cost = $26,000

Option B: $10,800 in payments, and the vehicle is worth $5,000, net cost = $5,800

In Option B, you saved $20,200. Now let's head over to the other mountain.

The *earn interest mountain* takes the $20,200 you saved by choosing Option B and invests it for the next thirty years. How much did you earn when that snow boulder hits the bottom in thirty years? The answer is $116,018. Knowing this—did the automobile in Option A actually cost you an extra $200 each month for an additional three years of payments? Or, did the option A automobile cost Future You $116,018 thirty years from now?

The Option B car will get you to where you want to go safely and consistently. You do not need the Option A car, but people make buying decisions based on emotion, not logic and people who understand the power of compounding interest earn it, while those who don't; pay it.

Here is the best tip I can give you regarding buying decisions. Hit the pause button.

How long is the pause? That's up to you, but I would recommend sleeping on it. Meaning, take a day and sleep that night and see how you feel about the decision in the morning. Take time to reflect and also project into the future. What will this purchase get you, and what will it cost you? Then, act accordingly.

Salespeople and billion-dollar marketing firms are well-trained professionals at making you feel like you have to act fast! They will give you limited-time offers with deals that will go away at the end of the day. They are playing off of the fear of missing out (FOMO), which creates an emotional reaction within you, causing you to make a rushed and poor decision. I'm here to tell you the truth—deals are always available. There will always be another limited-time offer. There are always options other than the one currently in front of you. Work hard to avoid impulse purchases today, and Future You will love you tomorrow!

Please allow me to wrap up this heavy math chapter with more math! Because I know what you are thinking; *Yeah, this all sounds great in a book, but none of it sounds fun in real life. I want to enjoy my life. I will work hard for my money, so I want to spend it and have fun!*

Well, here's the great news. . . I want all of that for you too. In order to accomplish it and still be financially responsible, you have to have a plan.

In life, people don't plan to fail; they fail to plan.

Here is one last mathematical equation I'd encourage you to use for budgeting. If you don't like mine, feel free to create your own numbers, but ultimately have a plan and stick to it.

10/50/5/5/5/25 = invest, bills, give, protect, emergency, fun

What in the world are those numbers? Glad you asked! Those are percentage allocations of your monthly income:

10% invest

50% pay your bills

5% donate

5% protect

5% emergency

25% fun

Let's say after taxes you take home $4,000 per month. This is what my equation would look like:

$400 into an investment, pay yourself first and add to that *interest earned snow boulder.*

$2,000 on bills. Pay your mortgage, rent, car payment, cell phone, monthly subscriptions, utilities, and so on.

$200 donated. Remember, those who always give will always have. Your generosity will come back tenfold.

$200 insurance. Have coverage to pay your bills if you become sick or injured and cannot work. Also, have coverage in place, so if you die before retirement, your family instantly gets what your snow boulder would have been at the bottom of the hill.

$200 into a savings account. Don't see or touch this account unless there is an emergency, such as—car repairs, home repairs, or unexpected bills.

$1,000 for fun! This is your money for the clothes, games, concerts, dining out, trips, and so on—just don't charge any of it.

Pro Tip: *Have separate accounts for all of these.* The more you can automate within your plan, the less you have to think about decisions. With separate accounts, you are less tempted to make poor decisions, and your likelihood of financial success drastically increases.

One final thought on this formula. You may think *$1,000 each month for fun isn't much. What if I want to take a trip that costs $4,000?* Well, keep it simple. You have two choices. Either spend less than $1,000 per month and save as much as you can in that account until you get to $4,000, or make more money. The more you take home each month, the more you'll have for bills, more expensive things, and investments—Future You will thank you. You'll be able to give more and feel greater fulfillment. Additionally, you'll have more protection and a bigger emergency fund. You'll invest more, and ultimately you can have more fun!

As humans, we tend to overcomplicate simple things. To be financially free, to live a happier, more fulfilled life and to do more fun things, do this:

- Spend less than you make
- Earn interest, don't pay it
- Follow the lessons of the *Essential F-Words for Teens* to continuously improve each day, and you'll increase your value to others which will ultimately increase your income.

Crossroads:

Every day you will be tempted to buy something you want but do not need. You have many choices at this crossroads. You can buy it with cash from your *fun money*. You can buy it with cash allocated to another account within your 10/50/5/5/5/25 monthly allocation. You can buy it with a credit card because you don't have cash. Or, you can pause, *sleep on it,* and determine if it's something worth spending money on in the morning. Impulse buying will satisfy you today but can destroy your finances in the future. I am not telling you never to buy things you do not need. I'm simply encouraging you to have a plan and think about how each purchase impacts your plan before you make financial decisions. Your future success and overall happiness depend on the financial choices you make today.

3 Things You Need to Know Before Graduation:

- Out of sight, out of mind—automate everything when it comes to finances.
- Resist temptation—have an accountability partner to help you with finances.

- Avoiding as much debt as possible before the age of twenty-five will allow you to live life on your terms throughout the prime of your career.

Section Summary:

When it comes to finances, you can earn interest or pay interest. It's crucial to have a plan. Specifically, one that includes investing while you are young—like now! Live below your means; focus on assets over income. Understand that you are your greatest asset. Know that the biggest advantage you have over those who are older is time, so don't waste it. Avoid the debt snowball. It takes very little time and effort to accumulate debt, but it can take your entire life to dig out of it.

We'll talk more about the basics around finances and help our Tribe of Teen members live a happy, healthy, wealthy life at www.tribeofteens.com

Section 8
FITNESS

Chapter 29
You Are What You Eat

"Good health is a crown on the well person's head
that only the ill can see."
~ Robin Sharma

Health is your greatest wealth. That sentence rhymes, sounds catchy, and most people nod their heads in agreement when they read it, but the reality is our daily actions typically do not correspond with our belief in that sentence. Here is the problem—especially at your age—it is unnatural to face your mortality. Chances are, as you read this, you are healthy and strong. You have countless years ahead of you to live life to its fullest. You can probably name a grandparent, great-grandparent, aunt, or uncle who lived to be one hundred years old. Through the lens of a teenager, one hundred years is an eternity. So, while you believe that your health is important, you carry a stronger set of beliefs that you'll always be healthy, you'll never get sick, and you'll never die. And, if you gain extra weight, become out of shape, or even battle a minor sickness—in your head, you'll have plenty of time to correct it. I know this because I had those same thoughts in my teens, twenties, thirties, and now my forties. This is a battle that, frankly, I've been fighting my entire life.

Where is the line between a focus on fitness and YOLO Syndrome? If you don't know it, YOLO stands for you only live once. The focus fitness side of me says, "Get up, get active early, do cardio daily, lift weights, and eat healthily. The YOLO side of me says, "Skipping the workout today won't kill you; your body needs rest and Scott, you only live once, so eat the pizza and drink the soda. You can work it off tomorrow."

But here is the deal, and it's a guiding principle known by all of the happiest, healthiest, wealthiest, and most successful people on the planet. Every thought leader and personal development guru has shared and practiced this principle. You will learn over two hundred thoughts, ideas, and mindsets that will change your life forever in this book, and by becoming part of our Tribe of Teens, you will receive thousands more in the future; however, this one principle, carried out with consistency will take you to wherever you choose to go physically, mentally, and financially. It's the *compound effect*. Sound familiar?

Every single choice you make will compound over time and determine your future. Since this is a chapter on physical health, let's stick with the theme. Will eating clean, healthy, fresh food from the earth today make you healthier immediately? Not necessarily.

Will eating fast food burgers, fries, and drinking soda make you unhealthy immediately? Not necessarily.

And there lies the problem. Because we do not receive immediate results, we do not believe our daily actions matter. However, with every daily choice you make, you are casting a vote. Simply put, if you eat healthily, you are voting for a healthier version of you in the future. If you make poor food choices, you are voting for an unhealthier version of you in the future. The same works when you don't choose—because you are still choosing by default. The problem is you cannot see the updated voting results in live time. You'll get the results all at once, many months or sometimes even years in the future.

Let's take a one-year time frame. Over the next three-hundred-sixty-five days, you are going to cast one vote each day. On average, there are thirty days in each month. What if you ate healthy three days each week? That's about twelve days each month. Not too shabby, right? When we carry that math out to the end, one year from today, you would have cast 144 votes for healthy you and 221 votes for unhealthy you. All along, you thought that making good food choices three days a week was a good thing, but you were ignoring the bad choices four days a week. When these numbers are compounded over time, even just one year later, unhealthy won by a large margin. What if we carry these numbers out for the next ten years? Healthy 1,440 versus unhealthy 2,210. Consider what it might be like fifteen years after that when you hit your forties. Healthy 3,600 versus unhealthy 5,525. And this example uses voting healthy three days each week. Just imagine what the results would look like if you made poor food choices five, six, or all seven days in a week.

I realize that I got heavy on math again, but the main point to digest here—pun intended—is this. . . every choice you make or don't make matters. It may not matter immediately, but those choices are votes, and they accumulate or compound over time. In your future, the results of how you voted will determine the person you've physically become.

There are currently close to one million books on the market today on the subject of diet. My good friend and physical therapist Todd Robbins—the twin brother of Travis Robbins, who wore my #3 jersey in that football game—tells his patients, "Every human is different. We all have different DNA. We all have our own unique blueprints. Health and longevity are not one size fits all."

I am not an expert on physical health, but I am good at simplifying complex problems. So here are five simple tips and strategies from me to you so you can avoid reading all one million books on the market.

Eat Clean: Ask yourself, "Did this product come from the earth? Is it natural? Do I know what the first ingredient listed is?" Or ask, "Was this manufactured or processed in a factory? Is the first ingredient a word I may have heard in science class but have no clue what it is?" Eat clean, natural food as much as possible.

Drink Water: A simple rule of thumb for water consumption is to take your current body weight and divide that number in half. Now take that number and consume that many ounces of water each day. Just like all beautiful things on our planet, flowers, trees, grass, lakes, and animals, you need water and lots of it. Often when you feel hungry, you are actually thirsty. Drinking water consistently throughout your days will curb your appetite.

Fast: Admittedly, it took me a long time to accept the health benefits behind this one. Your diet focuses on what you eat. Yes, that's important. But fasting focuses on when you eat, which is even more important. Without getting too geeked out in medical stuff, the basic premise is that your body creates insulin every time you eat. Your body also uses energy to burn things in this order: sugar, calories, and fat. If you do not eat for sixteen hours at a time—you can still consume water, tea, or black coffee—your body creates less insulin and focuses on burning fat first. Assuming you sleep seven or eight hours each night, fasting for sixteen hours isn't as hard as you think. Wake up and consume water, coffee, or tea until noon. Then, eat a clean lunch, consume healthy snacks, eat a clean dinner, and stop eating by 8:00 p.m. That sixteen-hour window without food from 8:00 p.m. until noon the next day will change your health forever when compounded over time. Side note, whichever sixteen-hour window you choose is fine. Perhaps you are more comfortable with 11:00 a.m. to 7:00 p.m. or 10:00 a.m. to 6:00 p.m. You do you! Just focus on being the best possible version of yourself.

Avoid Processed Food: I know I just covered this, but I cannot stress how important this one is. The human body was not designed to eat everything you see in grocery stores, restaurants, and especially fast food chains. Yes, I realize this is an area where we failed you as parents. Fast food was often convenient, and they certainly knew how to make it tasty. However, as you enter adulthood, now the choice is yours. I challenge you to be aware of what you are putting in your body. An old cliché states, "You are what you eat." Translated, I read that as, "When you eat junk food, your body becomes junk." And conversely, "When you eat clean and healthy, your body becomes clean and healthy."

I'll close this thought with another great one-liner from my friend Todd Robbins who always reminds me, "You can't outrun your mouth." Meaning we can't consume a fast food burger, fries, and sugary drink—

over 2,000 calories—then justify it because we took a three-mile jog which burned 289 calories. The math just doesn't work.

Cast More Healthy Votes Than Unhealthy: All positive choices start with awareness. Be aware that every choice you make matters when it comes to food and drinks. Read the labels, and know what you are putting into your body. Take that three-second pause to determine whether it's a vote for healthy you or unhealthy you. You only get one body and one opportunity to take care of it so you can enjoy as many years as possible during your amazing life. It's awesome to surround yourself with friends and family, have strong finances and build the foundational habits required to live a fantastic, fulfilled life, but if you ignore your fitness, none of it matters if you aren't around long-term to enjoy the fruits of your labor.

Please allow me to pause here with a reminder that nobody is perfect when it comes to healthy eating. In fact, I don't think anyone should be. Remember, with everything you do, strive for improvement, not perfection! Every once in a while, eat the cake, enjoy the donut, and drink the soda. Periodically reward yourself. The key is to consistently cast votes for *healthy you* each week.

Crossroad:

You are going to hit this crossroad at least ten times each day! You packed a lunch, but your friends at work want to order out. You go to a party, and there will be plenty of processed foods and sugary drinks. You know you should drink the water, but you just rather have something else. All day long, you will face food crossroads. And, you are in a society designed to lure you in and tempt you to make bad choices. You'll see television commercials, drive past fast food locations, and smell the aroma of sweets. It is not easy to consistently make healthy food choices. However, long term. . . it's worth it!

3 Things You Need to Know Before Graduation:

- Both good and bad food and drink decisions compound over time. Because we don't see the positive or negative benefits immediately, we don't realize they are there, but they are. Every moment and with every choice, you vote for your future health.
- Water, water, water. When faced with multiple drink options, choose water as often as possible.
- Give intermittent fasting a try. Eating during an eight-hour window and not eating in a sixteen-hour window has amazing health benefits.

Chapter 30
You Own a Super Machine

You heard me mention the name Todd Robbins in the last chapter as I shared with you a few of his golden nuggets regarding fitness, diet, and the human body. I am certainly not an expert in that field, but I am good at delegating things to others when I need help. After a recent round of golf, I asked Todd if he would contribute one chapter to this book to help you understand how precious your health is, the amazing capabilities of your body, and why you need to keep it healthy. Todd has studied physical therapy and the human body his entire adult life. Today he owns several physical therapy clinics throughout the state of Pennsylvania, and over the past two decades, he's helped tens of thousands of people recover from injuries and ultimately perform at a higher level. Without further to do, I turn this chapter over to Todd Robbins so he can share his knowledge with you.

What do you think is the most important thing you own? This answer will be different at different times of your life. At one point, I thought the most important thing I owned was a He-Man action figure toy. In high school, my first truck was the most important thing I owned.

The truth is that the *things* you own can easily be taken away. Sadly, I cannot find that muscular He-Man toy or his amazing Battle Cat anymore. I cracked the engine block on that Jeep during college and haven't seen it since. *The most important thing you will ever own is your body.* It is the most amazing machine that has ever been created. Unfortunately, most people have a deeper understanding of how to take better care of their cars than their bodies.

I want to tell you so many things about your body, but Scott only gave me one chapter, so I need to say more with fewer words. The body you have today has been developed over millions of years and battle-tested by evolution on our planet. There are more neurons in your brain than stars in the known universe. Your body has more computing power than the world's most powerful computer at the moment. No two bodies are exactly alike, so the body you own right now may be the most unique thing on the planet. In fact, your body is unique when compared to the other seven billion other bodies on earth right now.

Most people take the amazing machine they have been given for granted. It is incredibly durable and performs well even when neglected. Many of my patients end up in my office because they don't know how important it is to maintain the physical health of their bodies. If you misuse your powerful super machine over and over, eventually, it will break down, and you will need help to get back on track. However, even after years of abuse, the human body does a fantastic job of healing with the right guidance and behaviors.

I want to pass on a story that I ignored when I was younger, and most people do. I'll bet you are going to be smart enough to listen, though. Remember when you turned sixteen and you learned to drive? I bet your Mom and Dad helped you out a bit, and you got a car. Your first car is something you will always remember; mine was a white 1988 Jeep Cherokee. I spent hours washing that car, changing the oil, and doing my best to take care of it. However, as I grew older, I became a little less interested in car maintenance, and after all, cars are replaceable. I knew I could always get new parts or even a new truck if I needed to. Still today, I don't pay too much attention to vehicle maintenance, my truck now has almost 250,000 miles, but it starts every morning and gets me where I need to go.

Imagine how you would treat your car if the situation was different. Let's say you were given your first car on your sixteenth birthday. You get to pick out a brand-new one. Any one you want! Pretty good deal, right? It comes with one key caveat, though. . . this will be the only car you can own for the rest of your life.

How well would you treat that car?

Knowing that you could never trade in that car changes how you would treat it. You need it to last for the next sixty-plus years and get you where you want to go. You can replace parts, but the older your car gets, the harder it might be to do that. Also, when your car gets really old, it becomes a classic car, and the parts you'll need will be even harder to find; the mechanics qualified to fix that car will also be hard to find. If you knew you would only get one car for the rest of your life, how would it affect how well you took care of it?

When you were born, you were given the greatest gift the world has ever seen—your body. If you take care of it, it is designed to last you one hundred ten years. Sadly, people start coming to see me when their bodies stop performing well and begin to break down. Unfortunately, every year the clients walking into my doors are younger; it's disappointing. I now have patients in their forties and fifties getting new parts put into their bodies—from joint replacements to organ replacements. That is comparable to replacing major systems in a car—like the suspension and even the engine when the car has less than 50,000 miles on it!

I can't teach you in so few words how to take care of the super machine you have been given; I just need to plant a seed. Endless information is available on maintaining all the systems in your body so you can keep it running for one hundred years. The most important thing to understand is that your body is the only super machine you are ever going to get. There is a lot of recent talk regarding how technology will advance to the point that it will be easy to replace organs, joints, nerves, muscles and even your brain. I believe we will never figure out everything about the human body because it is the most complex instrument ever seen. It is much easier to take care of what you have been given so that it will keep running your whole life.

When you are younger, you will feel like your body is indestructible. I enjoy treating teenagers because their bodies respond well and heal quickly. My teenage patients continually remind me of how incredible our young body's ability to recover from injury is. I know it's not easy, but I want you to look into the future and understand that you will eventually be in your twenties, your thirties, and, if the universe allows, your nineties and hundreds. My goal is to reach one hundred eleven. Once you get there, you'll have the same body as you do today.

I want to impress upon you that life is a marathon, not a sprint. Actually, life is an ultra-marathon that you should plan on running for one hundred plus years. Most of my patients don't grasp the fact that they will have this same body, in some form, until it quits on them. They drive their cars as if they can trade them in for new ones. Unfortunately, the human body is much more complicated than your car.

The body you have today tells the story of what you have done with it for however many years you have been driving it. The same will be true when you are twenty, fifty, and one hundred years old. Everything you do and put into your body will result in the type of performance you get out of it. If you put good fuel, oil, and other fluids in the vehicle, it will run better. If you do the little things consistently to keep it clean and running well, it will. If you pay attention to the dashboard and listen to what the vehicle tells you, it will let you know when to take it in for maintenance.

If you ignore all these things and drive the car like you stole it, you are going to run it into the ground, and right now, you can't buy a whole new body, so you are stuck with it.

Crossroad:

Every moment of every day, you make decisions about what to do with the most amazing super machine ever built. All of those decisions affect the performance of your vehicle over time. What kind of fuel are you going to put in it? Choose a healthy diet.

Are you going to keep the fluid levels where they need to be? Choose to hydrate.

Are you going to make sure you don't drive it at full speed all the time and give it rest when necessary? Choose physical fitness and recovery.

Are you going to make sure you have a great mechanic you can trust to help you when simple maintenance isn't working? Choose excellent medical professionals.

These are all things you need to do now to have the body you want when you are one hundred years old.

What kind of car do you want to have eighty years from now? You get to choose. Each day you are in control of making choices that will affect how that car looks and performs. Make good choices.

3 Things You Need to Know Before Graduation:

- Everything you do with your body today sets the course for your future body.
- Life is a marathon, not a sprint. This is an endurance challenge.
- The only person who is really in charge of the maintenance of your body and how it works is you. Get guidance from other professionals, but you are the person making the small daily decisions that result in what your body will become.

Chapter 31
Anxiety

"Fear and anxiety many times indicates that we are moving in a positive direction, out of the safe confines of our comfort zone, and in the direction of our true purpose."
~Charles F. Glassman

I've battled anxiety since I was your age. I've experienced all different versions and levels of intensity at various times. For years I was embarrassed and ashamed of it. I felt it made me weak or that something was wrong with me because everyone else seemed fine. So, I did the worst thing a person struggling with anxiety can do; I hid it.

Certain chapters in this book will resonate with you on different levels at various times throughout your life. Perhaps anxiety isn't something you are dealing with now, but I can assure you that it will be present in your life in the future, and that's okay. Learn about it, learn to welcome it, and most importantly, talk about it.

In a May 11, 2020, article in the Harvard Business Review, they state that anxiety is the most common mental illness, affecting more than forty million adults each year. Close to 30 percent of Americans experience clinical anxiety at some point in their lives. According to the Institute for Health Metrics and Evaluation, an estimated 284 million people had an anxiety disorder in 2017, making it the most prevalent mental disorder worldwide.

Why is this? You have to understand that the standard brain equipment installed in you at conception is outdated. This is no fault of your own, but as the world has evolved, our brains have remained primitive. The primary purpose of your brain is to keep you safe and run efficiently. During the era of cave people, this was great. They slept or rested for twenty hours a day, then hunted and gathered for the rest of their time. While out and about, if they heard movement in a bush, their brain sent a message of fear, creating awareness of a potential saber tooth tiger. Fortunately, the chances of us being attacked by a tiger have significantly decreased nowadays! However, in this modern society, we have the same brain, and it's on overload. Instead of resting for twenty hours, it seems like we are on the run for twenty hours each day. Instead of sending fear cues to keep us safe, it sends us fear signals regarding homework, projects, assignments, making money, paying bills, balancing schedules, keeping people around us happy, our health, and the list goes on and on. What does it all add up to? Anxiety.

Anxiety comes in two forms: *facilitating and debilitating*. Also, understand that anxiety has no cure. It will always be in you, just not always noticeable.

Facilitating anxiety can work as a positive force within you. When you learn to recognize and harness it, you become more focused and energetic before a big event, such as a presentation, performance, meeting, or date.

Debilitating anxiety is facilitating's drunk brother that nobody wants at the party. It creates intense levels of fear about everyday situations to the point that you cannot even do certain things or function at all. For me, this commonly occurred when I was in small spaces or felt trapped. My entire college career, I couldn't sit in a classroom without windows because I freaked out. To this day, I struggle to sit in a car on the highway because I feel trapped.

Journey with me back in time onto my college campus, and I'll share an example of both types of anxiety. The first, debilitating, occurred in one of those closed-door classrooms without windows. I was sitting in the middle of the room and felt trapped. My heartbeat became noticeably faster; in fact, I could feel each beat in my chest. My breathing became shorter, beads of sweat formed on my forehead, and my hands began to shake. The shortness of breath caused me to become lightheaded and dizzy. I couldn't swallow and knew I had to get out of there. I also knew there was no legitimate reason this was happening. All I had to do was sit at a desk and listen to the professor. The fact I didn't understand why this was happening made things even worse. I frantically scanned the room, focused on my breathing, and tried not to fall onto the floor. I desperately wanted to leave, so I did. Abruptly I stood up, left my books and backpack behind, and stumbled out of that room—never to return. I dropped the class because I was scared to death that my body would respond the same way the next time I tried to sit in that room.

How about an example of facilitating anxiety now? Different classroom, stressful assignment—public speaking. Experts say public speaking is actually a bigger fear than death for humans. I wouldn't say I was scared to death, but I was definitely dealing with anxiety once again on the day of my speech. Fortunately, I had done some research and began learning how to cope with anxiety. I taught myself to recognize these scary emotions and translate them into excitement. Prior to the speech, I performed a series of deep breathing exercises and told myself to get motivated by these feelings of excitement.

In both scenarios, I had anxiety; one was debilitating, and the other was facilitating.

This is a deep subject and one we will consistently cover on our *Tribe of Teens* website and podcast. More than anything, my wish for you is that you understand anxiety is always present, it's nothing to be ashamed of, regardless of intensity, and it's essential to have somebody to talk to about it. Understanding anxiety and harnessing its positive powers will serve you well throughout your life.

Crossroad:

You will speed into intersections of life and suddenly be derailed by angst, worry, and overwhelm. You will feel short of breath, begin to sweat, and notice your heartbeat pounding through your veins. Anxiety can hit you quickly; it's often triggered instantly, like a light switch turning on. Unfortunately, it's not as easy to turn off. At this crossroad, become aware of your situation and understand this is a temporary state.

Focus on your breathing by implementing a technique that soldiers and police officers use before entering life-or-death situations called *combat breathing*. Deep breathing helps you focus and reset your body. The technique is simple. Breathe in through your nose for a three-second count, hold your breath for a three-second count, and exhale through your mouth for a three-second count. If you are in a situation where you can do this with your eyes closed, then close them. If not, no big deal. Repeat this nine-second breath pattern as long as it takes to decrease your heart rate. In through the nose for three, hold for three, and out through the mouth for three. I've used this before and during exams, prior to sporting events, presentations and during social interactions.

3 Things You Need to Know Before Graduation:

- Anxiety is natural, and it's normal. It's not something to hide from or be ashamed of.

- Remember the E + R = O formula here—events plus response equals outcome. We cannot control the event—anxiety. We can control our responses through awareness, breath work, or talking it through with somebody. The outcome will be just fine. In fact, you'll be stronger for having worked through it.

- Not all anxiety is bad. Our first essential F-word was failure. With failure comes anxiety. It happens before stepping out of your comfort zone and then again after you unsuccessfully try. Do not allow anxiety to keep you from trying and trying and trying again. Whatever is wildly important to you, do it. Harness your anxiety. Use it as a reminder that you are doing difficult but necessary work.

Chapter 32
Social Media

"Believe nothing you hear, and only one half that you see."
~from the short story "The system of
Dr. Tarr and Professor Fether"

Welcome to the land of make-believe. Here in social media land, people use filters to improve their appearance in an effort to impress people they don't like. They spend money they don't have to buy things they don't want just to post on social media in an effort to wow people that could care less about them.

Social media is a highlight reel. You see—the very best moments of somebody's day. What you don't see are the events happening behind the scenes or everything that led up to that moment.

Yes, I'm on social, and I realize in today's day and age, you almost have to be. However, I ask you to understand that when a product has no financial cost, *you are the product*. Social media was created to own, control, and manipulate you. Our newsfeeds look completely different based on our interests and hot buttons.

I intentionally placed this chapter immediately following anxiety. You may believe that social media is a solid downtime activity. Or a way to relax and take your mind off of your problems. The problem is it's creating more problems than you may realize. Limit your social media usage to less than an hour each day. Also, build in *detox blocks* where you totally eliminate social media for a day or two at a time. Not only will this reduce your anxiety by keeping you away from the comparison trap, but it will also take your eyes off content specifically placed there to manipulate your emotions. By limiting and, at times, eliminating social media, you will be more present throughout your day to see things that are real.

In place of digital distractions, create healthy distractions. These are things that require your full attention and complete focus. This way, your mind doesn't have time to think about anything else, allowing you to detach and recharge. Examples of healthy distractions include kickboxing, dancing, playing with children, puzzling, painting, building or fixing something, meditating, and so on. Anything that requires your full attention and doesn't add negativity to your life should demand at least thirty minutes of your day.

Tens of thousands of amazing places exist on this planet to experience and enjoy. The one place you don't want to visit consistently is social media, the land of make-believe.

Crossroad:

You may already have a physical addiction to social media. And if you don't now, be aware that it can happen. All day long, you will be tempted to take a peek at social. When you find yourself at this crossroad, you have a choice to make. Remember, everything has a time and place and anything you choose to do always comes at the expense of something else. Choose wisely.

3 Things You Need to Know Before Graduation:

- Comparing yourself to others is never wise. Comparing yourself to false perceptions of others lowers your self-esteem.
- Don't judge others who look, act, and believe differently from you. Don't be jealous of those who seem to have everything you want.
- *Run your own race.* While you can love and support others running their race, ultimately, you can only control what's happening in your own.

Section Summary:

The key to living is to do it while you are alive. The key to staying alive is making health and fitness your main focus. Eat clean, choose water, care for your body, and nourish your brain.

Become part of a physical and mental health-focused movement with our Tribe of Teens group at www.tribeofteens.com.

Section 9

FUTURE YOU

Chapter 33
Attitude, Actions, and Effort

*"A positive attitude may not solve all your problems, but it will
annoy enough people to make it worth the effort."*
~Herm Albright

You are now in the ninth section and thirty-third chapter of this book. This tells me two things about you. One, you are serious about learning, improving, and becoming that one percent better day after day. Two, you truly love and care about the version of you that awaits this world in the future. By now, you realize one of the underlying themes to being who you want to be, having what you want to have, and living the truly rich and significant life you deserve, is patience.

One more football analogy—games aren't won in the first quarter. Do you want to be losing by two touchdowns after the first quarter? Of course not. Yet, while the scoreboard clearly indicates you are behind, you certainly haven't lost. Plenty of time remains. Life is no different, but your quarters are longer, which allows you more time to adjust, recover from failures and create momentum toward a comeback. So be patient, as all good things will eventually come to those who are.

Understand that oftentimes in life, your wins will be a result of your losses. Winning is easy. If all you ever did in life was succeed at your first attempt, what fun would that be? On the surface, you would think it'd be great. However, the only way to consistently succeed at everything you do is to only do the things you are already good at. You can master something insignificant, which doesn't fulfill you, and succeed every time. However, that complacent path leads to emptiness. You'll live a boring life where you don't *ask* people for things you want, you don't try new things that you may love, and when challenges present themselves, rather than risking failure, you just quit. During your younger days, you'll succeed at avoiding temporary pain, but by taking this approach, you'll have cheated Future You out of long-term happiness. Don't be afraid to take some chances in life. You'll learn something from every challenge you pursue. If you shoot for the moon and miss, you'll still land with the stars.

Here is the easiest way in the world to make yourself miserable— focus solely on your results. If you only judge yourself based on your outcomes, you'll be miserable for 70 percent of your life. Why do I say this? Simply put, throughout your journey, if you truly seek to become the most amazing version of Future You, you will lose more often than you win. As a basic rule of thumb, people who push out of their comfort zones and try something new ten times will not find success during seven of those attempts. That's a failure rate of 70 percent. If you only focus on results, you'll be upset the majority of your days.

But what if you focused on the only things you can control: *attitude, actions, and effort?* What if you went into all ten of those challenges with a positive attitude, took massive action, and gave 100 percent of your focused effort? Regardless of the result, you'll be happy because you tried your best and gave it your all. Ten out of ten times, this will lead you to happiness. Three out of ten times, it will lead you to *extreme* happiness due to your successful efforts.

Understand that Future You will not be determined by the results of your life but rather by your laser-like focus on how you approach the only things you can control: attitude, actions, and effort. Remain focused in those three areas, and results will always take care of themselves.

Billionaire businessman Mark Cuban once said that it only takes one great idea to change your life forever. The most famous example of this is Thomas Edison. You know him as the man who invented the lightbulb. However, you may not know him as the man who failed to invent the lightbulb over 10,000 times! During his childhood, one of Edison's teachers told him he was "too stupid to learn anything." Edison was fired from his first job because his work did not produce results. During one of his failed experiments with the lightbulb, Edison burned down his laboratory! Through it all, Edison focused on the things he could control, his attitude, actions, and effort. When asked by a reporter how he could persevere through 10,000 failures, Edison famously responded, "I have not failed. I just found 10,000 ways that won't work." If you want to experience a happy, fulfilled life, fall in love with the process of trying.

Edison understood that he had to fight through setbacks to accomplish something that would make Future Thomas proud, along with the rest of the world, who no longer relied on candles for light. Thomas Edison died in 1931, nearly one hundred years ago, yet we still tell stories about him and enjoy the product he worked tirelessly to create. Control only the things you can control, don't focus on results, and understand it only takes one big idea to succeed. Regardless of your outcome—this approach will lead you to the best possible version of Future You.

You Are the *Only* Person that Matters

At various stages of your life, you will have teachers, coaches, mentors, bosses, co-workers, friends, family, perhaps a significant other, and most likely children of your own. You'll have different feelings on different levels for all of them. However, none of those people will be more important than you. When you consistently show up as the best version of yourself, you inspire all those around you to become better versions of themselves.

You may be thinking, *Wow! That sounds incredibly selfish.* Well, I thought the same thing when I first heard this concept too. It was during my very first time on an airplane. I was with my father and clearly nervous because I had never been in an aluminum tube traveling five hundred miles per hour, miles above land before. I paid close attention to the pre-flight safety instructions—obviously. The flight attendant explained that if the cabin lost pressure, oxygen masks would drop from above. Adults traveling with small children should place the oxygen mask over their own nose and mouth *first* before assisting the children. Wait—what? Did they just instruct the adults to put their needs ahead of ours? Yes, they did. And here is why, if the adults took care of the children first and by doing so, they lost oxygen and fainted, how much help would they be to those children going forward? Conversely, by having the adults take care of themselves first, they could now help the children through the remainder of this scary situation.

Take that concept of self-care with you throughout your life. Taking care of yourself first increases your ability to lead, inspire, and improve those around you. And while all of that is taking place, you are patiently moving towards the best possible version of Future You.

Crossroad:

You will go through slumps in life. Many times, it will seem like nothing goes right and the world is against you. Chances are, you chose the results road rather than the attitude, actions, and effort path. Don't stress; each time you head the wrong way at a crossroad, you can always stop and change direction. Take that internal timeout or use that crucial three-second pause to re-route yourself from stressing about poor results to focusing on an attitude of gratitude. Read through your past positive journals and think about the countless ways you are truly blessed. Shift your mindset from *I have to do things* to *I get to do things*. An attitude of gratitude will never fail you.

3 Things You Need to Know Before Graduation:

- You'll never be mad about trying something hard.
- Don't focus on results; instead, focus on the only things you can control: attitude, actions, and effort.
- Self-care is not selfish. In fact, giving others the best possible version of you—past and present—is the greatest gift you can offer the world.

Chapter 34
Eliminate Two Words and Change Your Life

"The Procrastinators meeting has been moved to tomorrow."
~Unknown, but most likely true.

As you know, one of the major forces behind writing this book was my years and years spent working with adults who are desperately trying to improve. I asked myself, would these amazing people, essentially just struggling with the basics, be in their situation today if they knew the nine essential F-words back when they were teens? How much different would their adult lives be if they had the opportunity to join our Tribe of Teens?

Of all the self-improvement lessons they could have learned as teens, the one most adults need help with—is *time management.* We already talked about clearly defining the actions and activities most essential to you. You know what a winning day looks like. You understand the power of compounding results and the importance of stacking those winning days by only focusing on the essentials. Now I'm going to share with you one word—and it's not an F-Word—that will derail your time efficiency and add stress and anxiety to your life without you even realizing it. The word is *later.*

Yup, I want you to become a hater of the word later.

Why? Because if quitting is the easiest thing in the world to do, waiting until *later* is the second easiest thing to do. I've seen countless people live what I refer to as a "later life."

I'm going to start eating healthily. . . next week.

I'm going to start exercising. . . on Monday.

I'm going to go back to college. . . next semester.

I'm going to take that vacation. . . next year.

I'm going to change jobs. . . as soon as a better opportunity comes up.

I'm going to tell that person how I really feel. . . as soon as I get the courage.

I'm going to buy that house. . . as soon as I have more money.

I'm going to ask that person I really like out to dinner. . . when I think they'll say yes.

I'm going to volunteer at a non-profit. . . as soon as I have more time.

I'm going to spend more time with my family. . . as soon as I get all of my work done.

Do you see how we trick ourselves as humans? Never once during those "I'm going to" statements did you ever read the word later, but it's there. However, do you know what may not be there? Later itself. You see, that's the funny thing about *later*, some people get theirs, and some people don't. Often times the "I'll do it later" approach lasts for thirty-plus years, and then that person is gone, or their health is gone, or their money is gone, or the opportunity or person they were waiting for is gone.

I was so excited to share the experience of attending your first live concert last summer. Your mother and I took you to see The Dave Matthews Band, a band we enjoyed during our teen years. In their song "Cry Freedom," Dave sings, *"The future is no place, to place your better days."*

Remember this maxim, "The past is gone, and the future may never come, so the present is all we get. *That's why the present is a gift."*

Don't throw away your gift by waiting to open it in the future. This is another skill that I know you already have. I've seen you on Christmas morning and birthdays—you know how to open gifts immediately. You would never wait a week, month, or year to open those gifts, so please don't do that with your time. Always remember the greatest gift is the one received each morning. It's a new day filled with countless opportunities. Don't wait; open that gift now and enjoy your present. Don't allow *later* to steal any of your days. Hopefully, this book has taught you the following:

- You won't feel ready, and you'll want to wait until later.
- You'll never be 100 percent ready to do anything you desire.
- Taking imperfection action is always better than having a perfect plan that you never execute.
- It's okay to fail. In fact, it's where most processes start.

Please, ditch later. Identify what's most important to you today, close your eyes, hold your breath, and jump into it. Sometimes it will be scary, but I promise you'll figure it out. And after every jump, you'll look back with delight because you dared to make that leap into the life you deserve.

Let's discuss the second word that will slow you down in your journey toward the best version of Future You. This word we will discuss in a car, hop in; I'll drive.

Okay, we are on the highway now, traveling at seventy miles per hour. I ask you why you decided not to attend that college that you really wanted to attend.

You tell me, "Well, I was going to go there, *but—*"

Suddenly I slam on the brakes, and our vehicle speed drops to forty miles per hour. The person driving behind us slams on their brakes, honks the horn, and curses as they speed by. As I accelerate again, cars fly past us as I work back up to seventy miles per hour.

Sorry about that, son. Let's talk about something else. Tell me about that job you applied for. It seemed to be something you'd enjoy, and the pay was reasonable.

You tell me, "Yeah, it may have been a good opportunity, *but*—"

The car abruptly slows down again, so quickly that you have to put your hands on the dash to prevent your head from hitting the windshield. Once again, horns are blasting, people are yelling, and every other vehicle on the highway speeds on by as we try to figure out what's happening with our car and accelerate back up to seventy miles per hour.

"Gosh, I can't believe that happened again. How about we talk about something lighter? Music! You love to write lyrics for music. How has that been going?"

You begin to tell me, "I do love to write lyrics. It's something I was consistently doing for a while, *but*—"

Screeeeeeeeching of tires, horns blaring, cars flying by, you and I sitting on the side of the highway.

One of my many wishes for you is to kick butt in life. However, to do so, the first thing you need to do is kick the "but" out of your life. Typically, everything that follows the word "but" is an excuse on some level. When people are asked to explain why they pushed something important to them to later, the response starts with confirmation that they wanted to and finishes with excuses that come after the word *but*.

You are young, loaded with talent and potential, and your car travels fast on the highway toward Future You. Every time you wait until later or justify not doing something important to you by using the word *but*—your car slows down. While your brakes are burning, those who aren't waiting until later and have eliminated *but* from their vocabulary fly by you. When it comes to real-life driving, please be safe and maintain a realistic speed. When it comes to figurative driving on your life's highway, put the pedal to the metal and let it fly! Every car you pass has chosen to wait for something else or believed the words that came after *but*.

Crossroad:

The greatest possession you'll ever own in life is your time. Time doesn't care if you feel ready, lack confidence, or are scared. Time has no interest in your opportunities, bank account, or relationships. Time waits for no one; it just keeps going whether you are ready or not, with or without you. Tomorrow you will wake up one day older and one day closer to the end of the time you get. When you stand at the crossroad of "should I do it now or wait," just do it now. When that voice inside of your head tries to slam on your brakes with the word *but*, silence that voice. Whatever that voice has to say after *but* is a lie. And you don't have time to listen.

3 Things You Need to Know Before Graduation:

- As humans, we never think we have enough time in our days. We also believe our lives will never end. Both statements are inaccurate. Every day has plenty of time so long as you only focus on a few essential items. All lives will end, so waiting until later to do whatever it is you most desire is a long-term recipe for failure or disappointment.
- With every challenge we face, we have only two choices: make it happen or make excuses. Excuses often arrive after the word

but. Stop your sentence before you speak the word but. Whatever words you just spoke—own them—good or bad—and adjust as you move forward.

- Be where your feet are. Fully immerse yourself in the present. Whatever you are doing, *do it*. Avoid distractions or risk missing out on the greatest gift you are ever given at this very moment.

Chapter 35
Don't Quit

*"You don't lose if you get knocked down; you lose
if you stay down."*
~Mohammed Ali

Do you want to know why so many humans get to the end of their life and realize they aren't the person they wanted to be?

It's simple.

In fact, it's the easiest thing in the world to do. It takes no effort, zero skill, and everyone is instantly born with the ability to do it.

They quit.

Yup, those four letters, Q-U-I-T, have ended more dreams, crushed more hopes, and extinguished countless fires that once burned inside people's souls.

Anything worth having is worth working for. You will raise your hand and say, "Pick me" when exciting opportunities or challenges arise in your life. You will sprint out of the gate with that bright flame of desire burning within you. And then. . . the work will set in, and the work isn't easy. The work never stops. Then, the obstacles appear. You will struggle and fumble. You'll be tested and fail. Then the process repeats itself. What you don't know through it all is that you are outrageously close to where you want to be. But you don't know that. You cannot see the finish line, you're tired, you lose hope, and then you do the only thing that can prevent you from accomplishing what you started. . . you quit.

Please don't quit on your hopes and dreams. Please don't quit on Future You. This current version of you is already so amazing. At this stage in your life, you have accomplished so much, are loved by so many, and you're only just beginning. Future You can change the world by positively impacting and inspiring all those around you. However, you cannot become the best possible version of yourself in the future if you consistently quit today.

Each time you keep a promise to yourself, you grow stronger and gain confidence. You increase love and respect for yourself. You gain the courage to make even bigger promises to yourself in the future. Each time you break a promise to yourself, you take away a piece of the Future You that you desire to be.

Don't Quit, Adapt

Please take a moment to understand the difference between these two words. To quit is to leave a place or stop something permanently. To adapt is to adjust to new conditions.

Remember that our first essential F-word is failure. In that section, a key takeaway should have been that it's impossible to fail. The only way to truly fail is to quit. So instead, I want you to *fail and then adapt*. Your goal—that thing you want—hasn't changed.

However, the initial way you tried to get it didn't work. That doesn't mean you quit; it means you adjust your approach based on your new knowledge. It might take dozens of adaptations to ultimately achieve your goal, and that's okay. Adaptations create the journey, the fun stuff. Quitting ends the party.

Another F-Word that applies here is *finish*.

Finish what you start. Future You is counting on you. The "cookbook" to success—both personally and professionally—only has two ingredients: consistency and persistency.

Don't spend your time chasing the latest and greatest anything. Don't jump from one instant success empty promise to another. Instead, remain consistent with slow and steady, proven success habits. Review the Foundational Habits section and stick to those.

You can't just do something once or twice and say, "I tried." You must remain persistent with your approach. If your first two tries don't work, then try and try and try and try again. Re-read the power of compounding in the Faith and Finance sections. Persistence always pays long-term dividends.

Doors of opportunity open for those who consistently knock. And I know you know how to keep knocking on the door. You have had that skill since you were young. During your first trip to Disney World, at the age of six, you decided you had to have a Donald Duck hat. It wasn't just any normal hat, though. The head was white, Donald's big blue eyes rested on the forehead, and the hat's brim was this gigantic yellow beak. The hat looked ridiculous. I knew you'd never wear it again. It was expensive; the temperature was outrageously hot, your mother and I had been alternating between pushing your sister's stroller and carrying your brother all day, and all we wanted to do was get back to the hotel room. But there was a problem. . .a big problem. . . *you wanted that hat.*

Here's how that hot, sweaty, frustrating conversation went.

Me: You can't have the hat.

You: Why not?

Me: Because. Now let's go.

You: Because why?

Me: Because I said so.

You: (now with arms folded and pouting face) *I WANT THE HAT!*

Me: LET'S GO!!!

You: (now with your heels dug into the burning hot pavement) I'm NOT going. *I WANT THE HAT!*

Me: (body temperature approaching 212 degrees and head about to explode) TYLER, you are NOT getting the hat (and with teeth clenched) *LET'S. . . GO. . . NOW!!!*

You: No.

Mom: Just get him the damn hat!

Me: Angrily buying that stupid hat. Yes, the one you never wore again after that trip.

Consistency and Persistency

You had both as a kid, you have them inside right now, and you need to carry both with you into your adult life. Obviously, your approach needs to change. However, your desire to persist and never quit until you get what you want is the secret to success.

Crossroad:

Some things in life are easy to get. Others will require extended periods of effort and commitment. *Everything you desire in life is worth working for.* As that work becomes more difficult, monotonous, or mundane, you'll find yourself at this crossroads; you can push forward or quit. Quitting will always be an available option. Pushing toward something meaningful in your life may not be. Don't quit.

3 Things You Need to Know Before Graduation:

- Don't create long-term solutions for short-term problems.
- Quitting diminishes your self-worth and depletes your future potential.
- When you feel like quitting, understand that it's just a sign that it's time to adapt.

Chapter 36
The Journey

"You are what you believe yourself to be."
~Paulo Coelho

Perhaps the dumbest question you get in your teens is, "What do you want to do when you grow up?" Admittedly, I've fallen into this trap and asked the same question of kids your age too. The question assumes that there is an answer, and there's not. The reality is nobody knows. Far too many uncertainties and uncontrollable variables await each of us in the future. Plus, if we continually learn, improve, and evolve, our journey may take us to places we may not have ever known about, considered an option, or even exists at the moment.

By the time I turned thirty, I had worked seven different jobs and lived in nine different apartments, condos, and homes. I made money and lost money. I did work that excited me as well as work I wouldn't wish upon my biggest enemy. Through this journey of changes, successes, and defeats, I learned a little something about myself at each crossroad. I didn't realize it at the time, but I was assembling a version of Future Me, the person I would ultimately become. After my teen years, I allowed my work to define my success; I was chasing a unicorn—which is to say, something that didn't exist. Everything in life changes when you realize making the most of your journey is true success.

Spend less time stressing about what you want to do and more time on who you want to be. What does that best version of you look like? Don't stress about being there yet; appreciate where you are now. You are an amazing human, and now that you have been given these *Essential F-Words for Teens*, foundational habits, and tools to succeed, you cannot fail. Failure provides feedback. Use that feedback to continuously improve.

Failing doesn't make you a failure. Life is equal parts figuring out what doesn't work and what does. You only get one shot to become whomever you'd like to be, and you have limited time to do it. Take action. Go make things happen. Enjoy every precious moment your life offers along the way.

You are deeply loved by so many.

You're capable of accomplishing whatever it is you desire.

You are worthy of everything awesome.

Now you are prepared to determine your direction and define your destiny at each crossroad in life.

Crossroad:

"When you come to a fork in the road, take it." ~Yogi Berra

3 Things You Need to Know Before Graduation:

- You don't have to figure your entire life out by the age of twenty. In fact, I would advise against it.
- Self-discovery is often a painful process of trial and error. Frequently it's through our failures and figuring out who we aren't that leads us to who we really are.
- You only get to be a teenager once, so do it while you've got it.

You are designed to do the difficult.
Don't run from the daunting.
You live with a liar.
It's that voice in your head saying "You can't."
Silence that voice.
Dare to defy it.
Have the audacity to dream so big...
...that people laugh at you,
while you accomplish everything they don't.

BONUS CONTENT

The Five-Year-Old Boy with a Magic Bell

Eddie was a five-year-old boy who didn't care much for kinder-garten. Reading, writing, classroom rules, and leaving home each day weren't his thing.

One day, Eddie was outside during recess and didn't feel like play-ing with his classmates. It was hot, and he was tired, so Eddie drifted towards a tree near the playground and sat down. Less than five minutes later, he was sound asleep.

During that mid-afternoon nap, Eddie dreamed that he was visited by a man who was ringing a bell. It was a small bronze bell with a short black handle, but it was loud when rattled side to side.

The man who visited Eddie explained that if there was ever a time in his life that he didn't want to be where he was or do what he needed to do, Eddie could ring the bell, allowing him to skip that moment in time and fast forward to the future.

How amazing, Eddie thought to himself. *From this day forward, I only have to do the things I like!* There was one problem, though. Eddie suddenly woke up, and he was still under that tree at the playground. The man was gone, and there was no magic bell.

As Eddie walked back toward his friends, he thought, *Well, that stinks, it was just a dream, and now I have to suffer through the rest of kindergarten.* Four steps later, Eddie kicked something as he was walking, and the sound that came from the ground was a ringing. . . like a bell. Eddie thought he had a dream, but did he? He looked down, and in the grass, he saw that magic small bronze bell with the short black handle.

Eddie picked it up, closed his eyes, rang the bell, and said aloud, "Please let me be done with kindergarten." Suddenly, Eddie woke up the next morning, and when he went downstairs to prepare for school, he was actually gearing up for first grade.

Wow! This bell works. Eddie was super excited. After a few days, he learned that being a first grader wasn't much better than being a kindergartener. In fact, the work was harder, and he had less time to play. *Surely things will get better after elementary school,* Eddie thought to himself. So, he closed his eyes, rang his bell, and wished he could wake up in junior high. To his surprise, he did!

Eddie was suddenly twelve years old and in the seventh grade. At this stage in his life, he had a little more freedom from his parents, his group of friends had been narrowed down, and he had a better understanding of his personal interests. However, the school work was harder, the homework took longer, the sports teams were more competitive, and drama seemed to surround his friends each day. Eddie thought, *This is certainly better than elementary school, but still not where I want to be. High school must be the answer.* With eyes closed once again, he rang the bell, made the wish, and went straight to high school.

As you can imagine, upon arrival, Eddie found all of the same problems, challenges and struggles with everything high school related as he did in elementary and middle school. Eddie thought *You know what, I just don't think school is for me. I want to be an adult, get a good job, make money, live on my own, and finally be able to enjoy life.* Well, he had the magic bell, so he could do anything he chose, and he did.

The next day Eddie woke up as a twenty-five-year-old man with his own apartment, a car, and a day job. Every morning he'd rise, drive to work, perform at his job, drive home, and spend a few hours doing a few things he enjoyed and a few things he didn't. Eddie would go to bed, wake in the morning, and do it all over again. Every other Thursday, he'd get paid and use that money to pay his bills. The cycle repeated, week after week, month after month.

Five years went by; Eddie was now thirty. He had a few different relationships that started well but ultimately fizzled. His friends had all gone their own way with careers and families. After one particularly difficult day, Eddie silently stared at that magic bell. He thought to himself, *What if I could just get to retirement, but when I get there, have all of the money I would have consistently invested from ages twenty-five to seventy? I'll be a millionaire, I won't have to put in all of the working years, and then I can finally relax and enjoy my life only doing the things I want to do. I'll do things when I want to do them, and with the people I want to be with. All day, every day. Now that would be amazing.* So, he closed his eyes, made that wish, rang the bell, and woke up the next morning as a seventy-year-old, wealthy, retired man.

Eddie now lived on a beach, drove a convertible, owned a beautiful home, and didn't have to stress about work or money. Five years later, on his seventy-fifth birthday, he found himself in conversation with a woman named Sally. Sally's seventy-fifth birthday was the previous month, and she reflected on how her life seemed to go by so *fast*. She reminisced about all the fun she had with childhood friends in school and wished she still had the energy to play like they did back then. She flashed back to her years in college when she dove deep into the study of human psychology. Sure, the work was difficult, and countless hours were spent at the library reading and researching, but it led her to her passion, which was teaching. For the next thirty-five years, Sally was an outstanding teacher and community leader. She was loved by her students and peers. Sally went on to pridefully boast about her family. From the financial struggles she and her spouse fought through after getting married to the sleepless nights with their first child and then their second. "Nothing about raising the children while balancing my career was easy, but looking back, it was all worth it, and I wouldn't trade it for the world," Sally said with a smile. She went on to talk about the mistakes made along the way and how she wished she could take a few things back, but in the long run, it all worked out.

To wrap up her reflection, Sally shared that this new season of life has her and her spouse even more excited. After so many years of hard work with careers and raising children, they now enjoy the fruits of their labor here on this beautiful beach. And they get to enjoy it with their grandchildren too. Sally said her heart is full when she sees her children and grandchildren playing on the beach and enjoying a life she worked so hard to craft for them. What a legacy!

As she stood up to leave the party and rejoin her family on the beach, Sally looked at Eddie and said, "Many days seem so long at the time, but when you look back, the years seem too short, don't they?"

Sally walked away, and Eddie sat all alone on his seventy-fifth birthday. It was then he realized that in an effort to skip over everything difficult in life, he had also skipped over everything he desired as well. He had money, a house, a car, and his personal freedom. What he didn't have was much time left to live or memories from a life that he chose to fast forward to the end.

Eddie sat in silence and sobbed. Through his tears, he saw the small bronze bell with the short black handle. He spoke aloud, "Please let this bell work just one more time, as I only have one more wish."

Eddie grabbed the bell, closed his tear-drenched eyes, and shook it as hard as he could. He wished he could return to kindergarten and live his life as he should have.

Eddie woke up with his back against the playground tree on that hot day during recess. He looked at his arms, his legs, the clothes he was wearing, and the people around him. Eddie was a five-year-old boy again. With excitement, he jumped up, took four steps, and kicked a small bronze bell with a short black handle. Eddie picked up the bell, reflected for a moment and then walked it over to the trash can to dispose of it as he ran off to play with his friends.

Understand Temporary

Begin wrapping your brain around the fact that everything in your life is temporary. I realize this is difficult because you've only had a short time here on earth, and you don't remember your first few years. Everything in your life seems like an eternity, and the way things are today will seemingly be this way forever. In this closing, I'm either bringing you really good or bad news; *nothing is permanent.*

The reality is. . . *everything* in your life is temporary. Just look at our list of essential F-words.

Failure: Each one is a blip on your life's radar.

Faith: You have the ability to build your faith strong enough to last a lifetime, but it will be challenged and can certainly change or stop at any time.

Foundational Habits: If built strong enough, these can stay with you the second longest on this list.

Friends: They come and go.

Family: Yes, they will always be family, but they can come and go.

Forgiveness: Forgive and forget.

Finances: Are very temporary.

Fitness: Is outrageously temporary; what a difference two weeks can make. . . good or bad.

Future You: Spoiler alert. . . one hundred-twenty years from now, your temporary body will be long gone.

So, what's the point?

Don't wish your years away, and don't run from what's difficult. Start understanding that you can change everything in your life at any moment.

Step one is understanding and believing that whatever you are experiencing, good or bad, at this very moment is only temporary.

Chase what excites and inspires you. Eliminate the thoughts and beliefs that don't serve you.

Only one thing in life is permanent. The secret is to pursue your passions before that day *one* final event occurs.

Everything is temporary. Your nine essential F-words will be in constant movement. It requires mental toughness to check in with yourself daily and make necessary adjustments. This book was designed to educate you and create awareness surrounding these key areas. Remember, mastery is a myth, and pursuing perfection is a profound waste of time. The secret to success is confidence through continuous improvement.

The world is filled with billions of people who, on any given day, can be Eddie Excuses or Successful Sally, and you will be both throughout your journey. Challenge yourself to understand which is which and which you choose to follow for the majority of your days.

Also, know that the world is filled with retirees who have everything society perceives as *successful*. However, the one thing they don't have, which money cannot buy, is time. Millions of millionaires would trade every material possession they own for the opportunity to go back in time and do it all over again. You have time. Please do not waste it. Enjoy every moment of it. Never forget the five-year-old with the bell and that many days will seem long, but the years are short.

Thank you for reading this entire book from start to finish. I hope you found as much joy and value within these pages as I did writing them. Since three has been a common theme throughout this book, I'll close with three asks.

1. Keep this book close to you, and periodically visit a specific chapter. Just like the planet earth spins and seasons change, so will your life. Some of the words you just read may not have made a ton of sense to you at this very moment. However, I promise you that as the seasons of your life change, you'll be amazed by how these words help you understand and identify certain crossroads.

2. If you have the financial means and truly believe that the secret to living is giving, please pay these words forward by purchasing *three* additional copies and gifting them to people you care about.

3. Personal development and mastery of your life do not end here. You have now reached the starting line. Success is an everyday thing. Knowing this, I kindly ask that you join me on your daily journey by becoming a Tribe of Teens member! It only takes sixty seconds to register at www.tribeofteens.com, and I promise the value you receive from the content we share will allow you to become just a little better version of yourself every single day.

CONGRATULATIONS!!!!

You have now COMPLETED reading the nine *Essential F-Words for Teens!*

Reading a book 100% cover to cover is actually something many adults I know have never accomplished.

You now know the truth about **FAILURE**—it's NOT a bad thing.

You understand the importance of **FAITH**—believing good things will happen even when you don't know how, when, or why.

You are building **FOUNDATIONAL HABITS**—taking control of what you can control and consistently getting the little things right.

You can identify true **FRIENDS**—you become the sum of those you spend time with.

You have unconditional love for **FAMILY**—those who always have your back no matter what.

You see the value of **FORGIVENESS**—forget the past, and move towards a fantastic future.

You grasp the long-term approach to **FINANCES**—the power of compounding interest and the debilitating nature of debt.

Moving forward, you will focus on **FITNESS**—you get one mind and body; it's a work in progress, but it works better when well cared for.

You'll never stop working to create the very best version of **FUTURE YOU**—the choices you make today will create a happy, healthy, loving, and giving version of you that will live happily ever after.

Stick around for a few more pages to officially wrap things up. Then, join us in the Tribe of Teens, where new content will be released daily. The book was just the beginning. Our journeys go on forever. . .

The 117 Things You Need to Know Before Graduation— Shortened Version

1. Don't seek a guaranteed roadmap to success. Everyone's journey is different, as is everyone's definition of success.

2. Money is only worth having if you earn it by doing something you love. Don't do something you hate, and sacrifice time with the people you love solely to make money.

3. Just jump. . . and then figure the rest out on the way down. You will never be 100 percent ready to do anything. If you are 70 percent certain a change is required to move you closer to where you want to be, you're ready to make that change.

4. Success and failure cannot be determined at any point during a journey. It's only at the journey's end that determination can be made.

5. The only person who can accurately give you a grade is you. Applying 100 percent effort trumps any letter grade assigned to a temporary result.

6. Rarely is there just one answer to a question or one path to arrive at an answer. Life celebrates curious minds.

7. Complacency is the enemy of progress. In life, you are either growing or dying. You are improving or regressing. There is no middle. Remaining comfortable avoids growth and improvement.

8. Taking imperfect action before you feel confident is how confidence is built. The world is filled with two types of people: those who talk about making things happen and those who are actually making things happen.

9. Four words that will always hold you back are, "I already tried that." Those four words create a false illusion that there's only one way to do everything. If you tried and failed, figure out a better way and try again. Your goals in life are far too important to quit on. Never stop trying.

10. You cannot control the things that happen to you. Trying to do so will only lead to frustration and anger.

11. The only thing you have control over in life is how you choose to respond to each event.

12. Saying nothing is always smarter than saying the wrong thing. Pause. Take three seconds to give deeper thought to the words you speak. A three-second pause between an event and your stated response allows you to better control the outcome of every situation.

13. Who you were yesterday doesn't determine who you will be tomorrow. Only the decisions you make today will make that determination.

14. Your education doesn't end when you graduate from high school. Challenge yourself to be a lifelong learner. In fact, you need to learn more to earn more. You may think you aren't smart enough to do something. Nobody ever knew anything— before they did. Permit yourself to suck at new things. Nobody masters anything immediately.

15. Blaming others is simply a ploy to excuse yourself.

16. Both positive and negative results are often invisible at first. Everything you choose to do or not to do matters, and there are always positive or negative results.

17. When you truly believe in something or somebody with all of your heart, pursue that passion and protect your strong beliefs from naysayers. Not everyone will see, believe, or understand

your vision, and that's okay. In fact, that's what makes it your vision.

18. There is no such thing as overnight success. The actress, singer, or athlete who just hit the mainstream and is suddenly making millions of dollars didn't just start putting in the work recently; you just now are seeing the results of their work. They put in years of faith and grit to earn what they are now receiving. It wasn't luck. It never is.

19. When a window closes, a door opens. Seemingly devastating events will occur, and at the time, you won't be able to understand why, but they'll lead you to new opportunities.

20. Understand that everything happens for a reason, and very rarely, if ever, will you understand that reason when those things are happening.

21. We all have a recency bias. During a breakup, we think, *I'll never love somebody that much again, or I'll never find somebody that good again.* Yes, you will. When we lose a job or money, we think, *I'll never find a job that good or have money again.* Yes, you will. Everything in life is temporary. Be patient; the reasons why always show up in the future.

22. While the safe road is comfortable, it's lined with stories of people with unlimited potential and minimal results. The greatest factor any human has when it comes to investing is time. You are young, don't be afraid to take chances now. You have plenty of time to learn from failures and adjust as needed.

23. It only takes one great idea to change your life and potentially impact millions on the planet. Don't allow one failure to stop your pursuit of your one great idea.

24. Think of the world as a cave. When you scream a word into a cave, the cave echoes that word back to you. Whatever you

give, you get back. Take all of your amazing, positive thoughts and big dreams and scream them out to the world. The world will send more of the same right back to you.

25. You have the ability to write your own book. You determine all of your future chapters today; just spell out the specific details you desire.

26. People want everything immediately. Those who receive everything they want are those who patiently continue to put in the work despite the fact they do not see immediate results.

27. Faith is the deep belief you have in something or somebody. You must have faith in yourself. Telling yourself personal affirmations is faith in yourself. And the things you focus on, like your vision board, are the things you will receive or will become. Faith gives you the ability to stick with invisible progress consistently.

28. The daily tasks that don't seem like a big deal are the biggest deals of all.

29. Your choices around doing or not doing the little things send a message to your brain which validates the type of person you are.

30. Momentum is a powerful force you can harness by accomplishing little things as soon as you wake up.

31. Living an intentionally awesome life starts by becoming awesomely intentional with your morning actions and activities.

32. Build momentum each day by completing simple tasks which allow you to stack wins and build confidence heading into whatever bigger tasks come next.

33. Early risers get a head start in life. They are accomplishing goals, creating plans, and building long-term foundational success habits while others choose to sleep.

34. The greatest shortcut you can take is starting your tomorrow the night before.

35. Sleep shouldn't be trusted to luck. Make intentional decisions thirty minutes before bed to set yourself up for success in the morning.

36. Mornings are easier when all non-essential decisions are decided in advance.

37. Long-term success happens one winning day at a time.

38. Expect to experience highs and lows in life. The key is to ride the highs as long as possible and understand that the lows are only temporary.

39. Be present in each moment. You can't change the past; you can't control the future. All you'll ever own in life is the right now. Don't miss it!

40. You never know how to do anything until you do! Don't waste your time uttering the words "I don't know how." Instead, find somebody who does.

41. Once you have an idea of what you want to do, seek out people who have already done it and ask them to teach you. Don't feel obligated to remain close to childhood friends. People will change, you will change, and that's a good thing.

42. Many want to be the smartest person in the room; my challenge to you is to be the dumbest person in the room. You will begin to think and act like your friends do, so choose who you surround yourself with wisely.

43. Life is filled with peaks and valleys. As soon as everything starts going well, oftentimes, disappointment will follow. Don't stay in a valley for long; know that more good times lie ahead.

44. Surround yourself with people who put your needs ahead of theirs. And then reciprocate their goodwill.

45. Those who give will always have, and giving doesn't always involve money.

46. There are three types of people on this planet: energy vampires, energy angels, and ham sandwiches.

47. Your real friends are those who know everything about you and still love everything about you.

48. The average four-year-old laughs five hundred times a day. The average forty-year-old laughs fifteen. Have fun, and never stop laughing.

49. The only person you should ever compare yourself to is the person you were yesterday, and by yesterday I literally mean twenty-four hours ago. How you look, your job title, your bank account, your clothes, or the car you drive should never be compared to anyone else.

50. Gossip is the enemy of progress. You can spend your time speaking poorly of others, or you can be a kind, compassionate, loving human, but you don't get to do both.

51. Unconditional love is the deepest, most meaningful love there is. Allow yourself to care for another human at this level. It's equal parts scary and exhilarating.

52. Not all relationships are the same. You can like or even feel love for another, but those feelings can be prioritized. Don't treat all tribes the same.

53. Almost everything in life is temporary, including our actual lives themselves. A family bond is the closest thing we have to permanent. Care for those relationships above all others.

54. Things that don't get planned don't get done. Never assume something will just happen or come together. Actively plan the moments you most desire in life.

55. As humans, we don't want to face our own mortality. We say things like, "Nobody lives forever," but then we believe we will. Never pass up an opportunity to be part of a family tradition.

56. Take tons of pictures, print, and save them. Just like people aren't with us forever, traditions will sometimes end as well. The printed pictures you hold in your hand years later will help you relive certain moments and bring that joy back into your heart.

57. Regrets aren't bad, and we'll always have them. The key is to keep that list shorter than the list of things you don't regret.

58. That pause to process situations before you act will determine the depth of your relationships with family.

59. Not all members of your family will be good people. Not all members of your family will have your best interest in mind. If you are in an unhealthy relationship with a family member, know that you don't have to stay there.

60. We get limited years to live, but forever to be remembered.

61. The story of your family's past doesn't have to be the story of your future. You have the ability and every right to be The One who changes the family tree.

62. You get to write the story of your life.

63. People think others have things figured out, but they don't.

64. You'll believe when people wrong you, it's your fault, but it isn't.

65. When you have a "can't hurt me" attitude, a willingness to forgive and forget, and the ability to cheer on others in their journey, you can't be beat.

66. Every choice you make either charges or drains your personal battery life.

67. You cannot see the lessons in difficult moments as they are happening. Taking a moment to reflect afterward will provide your greatest education.

68. Deep breathing is the strongest charging station in the world.

69. Beating yourself up over mistakes won't change the mistakes.

70. Forgive yourself. Permit yourself to move on.

71. It's okay to dwell on things for five minutes, but not five days or five months, and definitely not five years!

72. Don't carry other people's wrongdoings inside of you.

73. Trying to figure out why certain people act a certain way is an exercise in futility, don't bother. Simply understand that "It's them, not you," and confidently move on.

74. Nothing will free your mind and soul faster than forgiving others, even when they may not deserve it.

75. 0 - 0 = 0. You cannot lose something that you never had. So take chances.

76. Don't be so hard on yourself. People like you more than you realize they do.

77. Life is way more fun when you pursue what you want versus making the best of what you're given.

78. Always pay yourself first. If you have $100 to invest each month, make that the very first "bill" you pay. Nobody is more important than you—or Future You. Invest in yourself financially first, and pay everyone else second. Have fun with what's left third.

79. The longer you wait to invest, the more painful it becomes in the future.

80. Time is the greatest asset you own, and no amount of money can buy it back. Leverage all of the time you have to invest. Start now, and don't quit!

81. Work with an investment advisor or financial professional to help you structure a plan that Future You will be proud of!

82. Dare to be different. When the masses are all walking to the left, that's a good sign that you should be running to the right! If you want the results that only ten percent of people get, you have to do the things that ninety percent of the people are unwilling to do.

83. Don't take financial advice from people who are broke. It's wild how many people in your life will act like experts and offer their advice and opinions on subjects they know nothing about. Seek out people who have "been there and done that" and ask them how they did it.

84. Out of sight, out of mind; automate everything regarding finances.

85. Resist temptation; have an accountability partner to help you with finances.

86. Be CEO of Me, Inc. And be proud of your bottom line.

87. Both good and bad food and drink decisions compound over time. Because you don't see the positive or negative benefits immediately, you won't realize they are there, but they are. And you are always voting for one or the other.

88. Water, water, water. When faced with multiple drink options, choose water as often as possible.

89. Intermittent fasting—eating in an eight-hour window and not eating in a sixteen-hour window—has amazing health benefits.

90. Everything you do with your body today affects your future health.

91. Life is a marathon, not a sprint. It is an endurance challenge.

92. The only person who is really in charge of the maintenance of your body and how it works is you. You can get guidance from

other professionals, but you are the person making the small daily decisions that drive results.

93. Anxiety is natural, and it's normal. It's not something to hide from or be ashamed of.

94. Remember the E + R = O formula—events plus response equals outcome. You cannot control the event. You can control your response.

95. Not all anxiety is bad. One of our essential F-words is failure. With failure comes anxiety. It occurs before stepping out of your comfort zone and then again after you unsuccessfully try. Do not allow anxiety to keep you from trying and trying and trying again. Whatever is wildly important to you, do it. Harness your anxiety. Use it as a reminder that you are doing difficult but necessary work.

96. Comparing yourself to others is never wise. Comparing yourself to false perceptions of others lowers your self-esteem.

97. Don't judge others who look, act, and believe differently from you. Don't be jealous of those who seem to have everything you want.

98. Run your own race. While you can love and support others running their race, ultimately, you can only control what's happening in your own.

99. You'll never be mad about trying something hard.

100. Don't focus on results; instead, focus on the only things you can control: attitude, actions, and effort.

101. Self-care is not selfish. In fact, giving others the best possible version of you—past and present—is the greatest gift you can offer the world.

102. As humans, we never think we have enough time in our days, but we also believe our lives will never end. Both statements

are inaccurate. There is plenty of time in each day so long as you only focus on a few essential items. And our lives will end, so waiting until later to do whatever you most desire is a long-term recipe for failure.

103. With every challenge you face, there are ultimately only two choices: make it happen or make excuses. Excuses often arrive after the word but. Stop your sentence before you speak that three-lettered word. Whatever words you just spoke, own them—good or bad—and adjust as you move forward.

104. Be where your feet are. Fully immerse yourself in the present. Whatever you are doing, do it. Avoid distractions or risk missing out on the greatest gift you are ever given at this very moment.

105. Don't create long-term solutions for short-term problems.

106. Quitting diminishes your self-worth and depletes your future potential.

107. When you feel like quitting, understand that it's just a sign that it's time to adapt.

108. You don't have to figure your entire life out by the age of twenty. In fact, I would advise against it.

109. The journey is often a painful process of trial and error. Frequently it's through your failures and figuring out who you aren't that leads us to who you really are.

110. The only thing standing between where you are now and where you want to be, are your thoughts. Be intentional with the stories you tell yourself.

111. You'll never get stressed out because you are doing too much. You'll get stressed out by doing too little of the things that bring you the most joy.

112. Confidence is built by keeping the promises you make to your-self.

113. Don't worry about what can go wrong; get excited about what can go right.

114. Become brilliant at the basics of everything.

115. Don't trust your memory. Keep a daily journal and take pictures of everything.

116. Always have something to prove. Live your life like you are down seventeen points in a game. Express love to your significant other with the effort you gave on your first date. Laugh so loud that others passing by will laugh with you.

117. You only get to be a teenager once, so do it while you've got it.

F – THAT!

The world is full of naysayers. It's easy to find people who will give you every reason as to why something won't work. Typically, it's a group of Eddie Excuses who have never accomplished much significance in their own lives. That little voice in the back of your head will want to listen to the people in this group. However, Successful Sally says, "F that!"

Having a dream is easy. It's in your head, it's safe, and you can protect it by not sharing it with the world. Dreams are great, but they aren't real. When you die, your dreams die with you if you never move them out of your head.

Goals aren't as easy. Transferring your dreams from your head onto paper makes them real. Now you can see them, feel that paper, physically touch that paper, and read those words. So can other people if that paper gets out; yikes!

Commitments are downright scary! This is when you take those dreams from your head, turn them into goals by writing them on paper and then share them with others as something you are going to do. This exposes your thoughts and dreams to the world and will unleash the tribe of naysayers who will gladly remind you why your plan will fail. Unfortunately, the first group of naysayers will be the people closest to you, like your friends and family. That voice in your head will tell you to listen to Eddie, your self-doubt will spike, and your natural tendency will be to give up on your dreams. You'll find plenty of ways to justify this decision, and once you give up, the group of naysayers will welcome you back to their reality with open arms. They'll think they saved you by helping you avoid inevitable failure, but in reality, they just extinguished a fire that was lighting up your soul. Now Future You has changed, and Sally is angry.

Here is a list of actual feedback I received from my friends and family when I made the commitment to write this book and create a *Tribe of Teens* website. Everything after the "—" is what Successful Sally responded with.

It's hard to write a book—**F that!**

Kids won't read a book—**F that!**

If they do read a book, they won't join your online tribe—**F that!**

What was so special about your childhood that people will care about—**F that!**

Just stick to working with adults—**F that!**

You can write it for yourself if it makes you feel better, but nobody will read it—**F that!**

You will never distribute 1,000,000 copies of your book to teenagers—**F that! Watch me!!**

15 Books to Read If You Enjoyed This One

The 4-Hour Work Week by Tim Ferris

The Slight Edge by Jeff Olson

The Secret by Rhonda Byrne

Everyday Hero Manifesto by Robin Sharma

Atomic Habits by James Clear

The Power of One More by Ed Mylett

Outliers by Malcolm Gladwell

Girl Wash Your Face by Rachel Hollis

The Happiness Advantage by Shawn Achor

How to Win Friends and Influence People by Dale Carnegie

The Compound Effect by Darren Hardy

The 7 Habits of Highly Effective Teens by Sean Covey

You are a Bad Ass by Jen Sincero

Tuesdays with Morrie by Mitch Albom

Essentialism by Greg McKeown

Shout Outs!

My Coach Brett Hilker. Thank you for your thoughts, insight, and encouragement along the way. You kept this project on schedule and challenged me to consider angles and approaches that I otherwise wouldn't have.

My Editor Amy Pattee Colvin. Thank you for being you. You are truly amazing at what you do. Somehow you moved into my head and helped me express my thoughts using far less words and proper punctuation—no small feat!

My Illustrator CJ Warwood. Thank you for taking my words and creating fun images. My drawing skills peaked in kindergarten. Without your contribution the readers would have received ugly stick figures from me.

My Brand Builder Ben Kolarcik. Thank you for helping me find my brand DNA. You are masterfully skilled at eliminating ambiguity. You have challenged me to dig deeper into my true purpose than ever before. I'm a better person for it!

My Everything, also known as my wife, Kelly. It's ironic the final words written in this book are to you because they could truly start a new book sharing our journey. I'm certainly not overstating when I say, "None of this would have been possible without you." And by *this*, I mean, Me, my career, our family and obviously this book. Thank you for always supporting me, offering grace when my mind is buried in projects and allowing the blocks of time required to be locked away writing. And thank you for sharing me with the world. Behind every successful man there stands a woman. Thank you for being my person. I love you!

My Super Fancy Bookmark

FAILURE—it's NOT a bad thing. Failures offer you feedback for future improvements.

FAITH—believing good things will happen even when you don't know how, when, or why.

FOUNDATIONAL HABITS—taking control of what you can control and consistently getting the little things right.

FRIENDS—you become the sum of those you spend time with.

FAMILY—those who always have your back no matter what.

FORGIVENESS—forget the past, move towards a fantastic future.

FINANCES—the power of compounding interest and the debilitating nature of debt.

FITNESS—you get one mind and body; it's a work in progress, but it works better when well cared for.

FUTURE YOU—the choices you make today will create a happy, healthy, loving, and giving version of you that will live happily ever after.